FREEDOM
TO
WANDER

Connecting with the Past,
Reinventing the Future

Robert M. Gaglio

ICT PUBLISHING

29 Strathmore Blvd.
Sarasota, FL 34233
ItalianCulinaryTours.com

Book cover and interior design by Monkey C Media
Edited by Jane Saxton and Meghan Hoch
Copy edited by Stephanie Thompson
Italian editing by Eugenia Angelini
Cover photo © 2019 Joseph Gaglio
Photos from the author's personal collection unless otherwise noted

First Edition
Printed in the United States of America

ISBN: 979-8-9889928-0-6 (trade paperback)
979-8-9889928-1-3 (hardcover)
979-8-9889928-2-0 (ebook)

Library of Congress Control Number: 2023915707

This book is dedicated to Kurt Alan Younker;
it was his generosity and genuine interest in me that created
a spark to change my life in ways I never could have imagined.

FOREWORD

There are four kinds of guides all over the world, two of them to be avoided. The first is a non-professional, a friend or acquaintance who wants to show you "his Rome," and largely ignores the very things you wish to see. The second is a hired guide who, over the years has spent too much time trudging through the same streets and churches so that he no longer sees them but only speaks about them and comes to believe the most dramatic of legends that seem to amaze his troupe.

The third is a professional who is often an art history professor or amateur archaeologist who seeks to fill every moment with more and more sights and sites while explaining every roof beam, every pane in a stained-glass window, and every crypt in every church. You certainly get your money's worth with such a guide but the cost of shoe leather and brain overload can set in after three hours.

The fourth kind of guide is the best: He or she is still passionate about showing off a city he or she loves, and, over the years, has accrued an appreciation for what the tourists in his or her care truly wish to see. This last kind of guide is never condescending, ever helpful in steering you towards the best and away from the worst places and restaurants, and paces the tour without fear of you becoming worn out by the experience.

Of this last sort is Robert M. Gaglio who was fortunate enough to discover his goal in life after years of working at a place whose very name suggests lethargic boredom: bank job. Like Dante, in mid-life, he had a vision of a vita nuova, first in Sicily, then in Tuscany, then everywhere else in Italy. And in the spirit of a convert, he found it necessary to share his enthusiasm, to change from being Dante to becoming Virgil. As he noted after one client expressed such deep-seated satisfaction on one of his tours, "Those days touched him and this convinced me that I could no longer wait until I retired ten years in the future to do this thing I was loving so much."

Robert becomes more of a Roberto the more he falls in thrall with the country, the people, and most of all, the food and wine of Italy, a love he was able to express to his clients as he himself learned more and more. As the child of immigrants, he carried his DNA proudly, and he found that there was a very good living to be made in sharing the good life with people willing to pay for it. I was so honored when he began showcasing dinners based on my book *How Italian Food Conquered the World*—a title I believe more firmly all the time.

Robert's book is, of course, a memoir as well as a testament to the old, very American idea of hitting the road. We get to share the last touching moments he spent at his mother's bedside before she passed away. Along the way around Italy, we meet the inevitable characters, like the whistling lady of Castelcivita, the butchers and fishmongers of Palermo at Mercato di Ballarò, and Sicilians who adopt him as much as he does them, and becoming a dual citizen.

Throughout this lovingly paced book, which, like a good guide, moves slowly and stops to allow the reader to marvel right along with Robert at his new finds, you range from the mountains to the shores, the villages to the cities, the trattorias to the ristoranti.

Freedom to Wander shows as much about the Italian way of life as it does about a rewarding personal journey. We should all be so lucky. In the meantime, we can let Robert lead the way.

—**John Mariani**, author of *How Italian Food Conquered the World;* former food and travel columnist for *Esquire Magazine* and former wine columnist for *Bloomberg News.*

INTRODUCTION

"Is this it?"

After all my years of effort, school, career, investing, and raising a family, I realized that there wasn't much joy in my life. I had done all the things I thought I needed to do to become successful and happy, but the results didn't seem to materialize.

Then I took a trip to Sicily to visit the birthplace of my grandparents. That trip proved to be a turning point. A new beginning.

Just a few years after that first trip, I led a small tour group to Tuscany. During that tour, the guide, Cristina, led us through the Siena Cathedral. As she spoke, I marveled at the beauty beneath my feet, where 56 marble-inlaid mosaic artworks covered the entire cathedral floor. Those artworks provide worshipers and visitors a representation of the sibyls, scenes from the Old Testament, allegories, and virtues.

One scene stood out to me the moment I saw it so I listened intently to the story Cristina was telling us, which I will paraphrase:

The "Mountain of Wisdom" shows the personification of fortune, and how to become wise. First, you have to be lucky, very lucky to be wise. Lady Luck, who has a wonderful, charming, young body, begins every human path, but she has no balance, nor stability. One foot is resting on a sphere, the second on a broken boat, and she is leveled by the wind and the wind has no real direction.

So, don't run after fortune if you wish to be wise. Don't run after beauty, money, or glory. What is another option? Climbing a very steep hill. It's not easy; it's very steep and full of obstacles and snakes. It is very hard, so people tend to give up; they look lost, disappointed, tired, and deceived. But if you keep climbing, reach the top, and get rid of your material wealth, then you are wise because you aren't bound to your wealth. You realize you are wise when you are stable, when you are peaceful. Peace is the real result of wisdom.

Cristina's words caused me to focus on my own life's path. The man at the top of the mountain tossing his basket of jewels, gold, and coins into the sea convinced me to think differently. This lesson from Socrates couldn't have come at a more perfect time for me. I would go on not measuring my success in terms of my bank account, but in ways that value time most of all.

I realized suddenly, with clarity, that peace was the most important thing for me, and having the freedom to wander gave me the opportunity to find it. This is what I had been looking for.

This was it!

Chapter 1

THE GENESIS

I am often asked the question, "How did you start a tour company in Italy?"

Freedom to Wander answers that question, but the short answer is simple: "It just happened."

It wasn't as if I sat at my bank job dreaming of starting a tour company. That was never the goal. In fact, I never thought that was even a possibility before I visited my family in Sicily for the first time. One thing led to another and then it all came together.

But if there is one event that led me to this industry, I would say it was the experience I had with my former boss at Comerica Bank, Kurt Younker. He'd rented a Tuscan villa and invited me to spend a week with his family in 2013. That was my first time in Tuscany, only my second time in Italy, but it revealed a path that would forever change my life in ways that I never could have foreseen.

God puts people in our paths for a reason, and I believe that Kurt was placed in my path to create the genesis for change in me.

A Man Larger Than Life

My first visit to Italy was in 2012. Although my mother was born in Sicily and my father was the son of Italian immigrants, I hadn't made visiting my ancestral homeland a priority. But I was coming up on my 50th birthday and my son had just graduated from high school, and we needed a special celebration. Maybe it was the fact that I was approaching the half-century mark in age, or simply the fact that I knew very little about my parents' families, but something called me to visit Sicily, and in particular the town of Montelepre, the birthplace of my grandfather, Francesco Gaglio.

Kurt Younker running with the bulls in Spain.

When I later told Kurt this story, he was very interested in my experience, probably because he was an avid traveler himself. Kurt and I had found ourselves in the post-Great Recession Florida banking world, in positions for which we weren't best suited, or at least I wasn't. I was in a wealth management office, but with responsibilities over the retail bank, and Kurt, an extremely successful wealth lender and manager, took on the responsibilities of the small branch banking network in Florida that was part of the big regional bank. The bank had taken huge losses in Florida and it was pretty clear its future growth plans didn't involve expanding in-state.

One day, after learning that I planned to return to Italy the following year, Kurt invited me to spend a week with him and his family in Tuscany. I was blown away by his offer and at first thought I couldn't accept it. But he insisted.

"We've rented a big house in Chianti and there's an extra bedroom and bathroom just for you."

"Did you ask your wife about inviting a 50-year-old, divorced guy on your family vacation?" (I've learned that husbands don't always ask their wives things in advance.)

He laughed, "Of course."

I accepted with one caveat: "Only if you let me be the cook for the week!"

That summer, I arrived in Italy and after a quick tour of Venice, I rented a car and drove to the town of Greve in the Chianti region to meet Kurt and his family. As I approached, I saw their beautiful stone villa on a large hill overlooking Greve. It was like something out of a classic romance movie, surrounded by lush woods on one side and a similarly spectacular view on the other. Summer flowers were woven throughout the grounds soaking up the afternoon sun. It was breathtaking.

The next morning, I was already anxious about my commitment to cook for Kurt's family. I enjoyed cooking for my own family but was taking a leap cooking for his, and preparing most of the dishes for the first time. I was excited to get started, so we made a list and Kurt handed me a pasta recipe. Then Kurt and I took off to look for the food vendors in the town of Panzano, just over the next hill. He was such a well-traveled individual that he researched everything down to the foods favored in the locations he visited.

Through the following years, I've regularly visited Panzano with my tour groups. Every Sunday morning, the town sets up an outdoor market with vendors selling flowers, vegetables, cheese, fruit, clothes, and kitchen items.

One of the reasons I love to schedule our Tuscany tours in September is that the grape harvest and wine festivals that time of year in Panzano are some of the best. The *Vino al Vino* (Wine to Wine) festival is held on the third weekend of September with a collection of 22 fabulous, mostly organic, vineyards and wineries. Guests love to participate in these wine festivals and enjoy the tastings of this Denomination Chianti Classico region.

On that particular Sunday, we took our list to the meat market, which I learned several years later was the very famous L'Antica Macelleria Cecchini, owned by the European celebrity butcher Dario Cecchini. People come from all over Italy, indeed all over the world, to eat, drink, talk, and just enjoy the scene at L'Antica Macelleria Cecchini.

Knowing nothing about his fame at the time, I looked up at the towering, stylish man, wearing an apron over his silk shirt, pressed slacks, and expensive leather shoes, and began to read off the items on my list.

Dario Cecchini, Macelleria Cecchini, Panzano in Chianti.

"Do you have any chicken?"

Now, he was already a tall man, but the counter and floor he stood on were raised about a foot from the store floor. From this vantage, he looked down at me with disgust, "No, just meat!"

Seeing his dissatisfaction with my silly question, I then asked, "Oh, do you have any pork?"

Now his dark eyes began to narrow and slice through me as he said, "NO, JUST MEAT!"

Then it hit me: "meat" in English to him meant only beef. I responded, "Oh, okay, can I buy some steaks?"

"Did you place an order?" Which of course I hadn't. Instead, I bought four pounds of chuck beef, which I cut up back at the villa, and some Tuscan salami called *finocchiona*.

I soon brushed off my feelings of Italian culinary ignorance and shopped for the other grocery items on our list. It was such a joy, visiting the little shops with their goods presented in such an artistic way and gathering the food I would use to create the dinners for this lovely family.

It was a little challenging, however, since their son didn't eat any vegetables or fruit whatsoever and their daughter was a vegetarian. But I managed.

It was glorious cooking in this amazing villa in the Tuscan countryside. The kitchen had a sturdy table, and despite it being an old villa, it had plenty of counter space. The massive wood beams in the ceiling and stone walls created a charming ambiance to prepare the meals. It was a perfect situation and by that first Wednesday I got the feeling Suzanne, Kurt's wife, was truly appreciative that I was doing the cooking and washing the dishes.

I was also included in some of the family's daily excursions. We visited San Gimignano, a small, walled village famed for its many medieval towers, then we toured Florence with a wonderful tour guide who showed us the many treasures of the picturesque city. I loved every minute so much that it gave me the idea to rent a villa with some friends the following year.

This is where I first learned to create an amazing villa experience for my clients and I am forever grateful to Kurt and Suzanne for allowing me to be part of their vacation. If that had not happened, I never would have started the tour business I so enjoy today. I've had hundreds of guests who have experienced this special part of Italy and I owe it all to Kurt for reaching out to me at a time in my life when I needed it the most.

Soon after that first trip, I devised my plan to come back to Italy the following year, but this time I would rent a villa and find friends to travel with me. To subsidize my travel expenses, I would coordinate all aspects of the trip and charge a fee to pay for all of the expenses. It was a win-win! I would do all the work: planning, making reservations for the villa and the van, lining up the tour guides and wine tours, as well as doing the shopping, driving, and cooking. All of which I loved doing. In return, the guests received an amazing Tuscany experience that was far less than half the usual cost.

Since I was in the banking profession, I knew several attorneys and other professionals who might be interested in experiencing a week in Tuscany. So, during my business calls, I invited several of them to spend the week with me. In no time, I was able to convince three other couples to join me for a week in Tuscany.

The rest of that year, I worked on putting together the tour. Kurt referred me to a villa broker in San Francisco who arranged the villa we stayed in the prior year. The broker didn't take credit cards and being a banker, I had reservations about sending a $7,000 deposit check without the protections of a credit card. However, I felt comfortable with Kurt's reference and mailed the broker the check. And so, it began.

Before I knew it, seven years in my touring business had gone by. I'd just had my best year so far and my first thought was to call Kurt. Although I had thanked him a few years prior, I wanted to thank him again. The cell number was no longer working, and thinking that was strange, I decided to email him. When several weeks passed without a reply, I was starting to get concerned. Then I received an email, except it wasn't from Kurt. It was Suzanne who responded.

"I am sad as I write this to you because I remember fond memories of our time in Tuscany as well," she wrote. "Kurt always spoke very highly of you and enjoyed your company. He was excited that you started your company after being inspired by our trip. Heartbroken,

I must tell you that Kurt passed away from a sudden accident in June of 2018."

My stomach turned upside down after reading her words. *How could this be?* Although he was only a few years younger than me, he was in perfect shape. Kurt was larger than life. I remember his travel stories, especially one about running with the bulls in Spain. He was the kind of man who left a lasting impression.

My heart ached from the news. This amazing man was taken from his family when his son was a senior in high school and his daughter was just starting college. I've been so blessed by the people God has placed before me and Kurt was one of the most influential. He'd given me the biggest gift a person could ever give: a path to find my purpose in life at a time when I was most disenchanted by life itself.

Kurt must have seen a spark in my eye when I spoke to him about my first trip to Italy and realized how passionate I was about the experience. Traveling with him provided the template for the tour that would reach the hearts of so many of my future guests. I can no longer thank Kurt in person, but he will always be a part of my life and career.

The Villa

It's funny how events unfolded. The villa I rented on that first trip ended up being the best one I could have rented for the tour business. Firstly, it's 500 years old and sits in the middle of a large vineyard with a breathtaking vista. It's so beautiful I often have guests stay behind for one of the tour days just to enjoy the view of the land, or relax by the swimming pool.

Secondly, it's conveniently located close to the *autostrada* (a major toll road) just southwest of Florence, giving us quick access to the airport, the city of Florence, and the freeway for tour days.

But the most important aspect of this villa is the couple who own it, particularly Loredana, who is responsible for running the rental business and taking care of the property. After all, it was her vision for the property that turned a rundown and almost unsalvageable house and carriage house into the charming villa it is today.

When Loredana and her husband purchased the villa, her parents told the young couple they were crazy for buying such a dilapidated and decaying property. This was before the movies *Under the Tuscan Sun* and *Eat, Pray, Love* created a worldwide desire to visit the Tuscan hills. These movies also generated tremendous demand for English and other wealthy European investors and second-home buyers to snatch up these properties that had mostly been abandoned by the local populations when they had moved to the cities for employment.

In the beginning, once the house was livable, the couple made it home for the next 15 years and raised their son there. Over time, the improvements began to take shape. A new roof and reclaimed river stone exterior replaced the old, crumbling stucco finish.

They reclaimed a large bedroom window that had been bricked in with a smaller window many years before. This created the best room in the house, in my opinion, with its now full view of the incredible vineyard and valley below.

They also brought in a massive amount of soil to create an area for the modern swimming pool. The grounds were landscaped with fruit trees, additional olive trees were put in to go along with some of the older ones, and classic Tuscan cypress trees were planted along the road to the property.

All the rooms were renovated, and additional bathrooms were constructed, all the while keeping the original farmhouse charm.

They converted the carriage house into two units—one for the couple to stay when guests were in the main villa and a smaller apartment their son could use when he visited. I sometimes stay in that apartment myself when we have tours there.

Over the years they have completely restored the property and are currently working on the second generation of restoration, removing some of the modern first renovations and replacing them with more traditional improvements, as well as the addition of a bathroom for the master suite and its king-size bed.

Loredana takes such great pride in the work they do while also following the strict guidelines required by the local government. For example, the new wall around the property had to be constructed with the river stone from the river at the bottom of the valley, which they had to physically retrieve.

The décor of the rooms and the renovation of the kitchen have created such an enchanting experience for guests who stay there. Each year when I return, Loredana loves to surprise me with the work they've completed over the winter, such as the beautiful renovation of the swimming pool that was completely restored with a perimeter of black granite, or the new fireplace with its reclaimed mantel from a nearby property. It makes for a gorgeous centerpiece for the sitting room where guests can read a book or play a board game. They have also restored the first floor which replaced their first renovated floor with more traditional and authentic Italian tiles like those used several hundred years ago.

Each room has been lovingly adorned with Loredana's marvelous taste in antique furniture. Some of the pieces date back many years and are from her own family.

Knowing this, I will never forget the horrific mistake I made by not using a cover for the kitchen table and improperly scrubbing the surface over the weeks, leaving it damaged. As Americans, I don't think we understand the concept of longevity when it comes to things like furniture. We live in a throwaway society with cheap imports to fill our homes. But that mistake taught me perspective. Beyond its aesthetic charm, the table conveyed a lesson in the Italian culture of keeping things intact over the centuries. In a culture that values continuity of everyday customs, an element as simple as a table serves to bond the generations, particularly elderly and younger people.

A few hundred euros later and a lesson learned, I came to deeply appreciate having the opportunity to live in such a home for the many months I've spent there.

That 200-year-old kitchen table is part of the soul of the home and has been a part of so many meal preparations in its lifetime, more like a family member than an inanimate object. I now see her as another tool in making the delicious meals we prepare for our many guests. I love the creaking sound she makes as I knead the pasta dough, and the support she provides for the continuous pushing and folding. Her grand spaciousness also gives us plenty of room for guests when plating each course of our meals and during our cooking classes.

The villa is the perfect home base for guests to stay and enjoy an authentic Tuscan experience. For guests who are looking for a slower pace, more nourishing meals, and meaningful experiences—the villa provides.

My first season there brought an epiphany. It convinced me that this was the place I needed to lease going forward. The experience of renting a minivan, driving my friends from town to town, shopping for groceries, and preparing all the meals for us that week will forever be one of my fondest memories.

In those early days, even though I was running on only four to five hours of sleep each night, the wine was so good I didn't feel any side effects as I started it all over again the next day. One evening, there was a moment when all my friends had gone off to bed and I was sitting under the arbor gazing up at the starry sky and the glowing moon. It was as if time were standing still, and a rush of happiness overtook me. I knew from that point on that I had to follow this passion and share this experience with as many people as possible.

By my second tour trip, Kurt's boss Angela (the president of the bank's Florida operations) and her husband, Anthony, became my first official clients for the Tuscany tour. I essentially ran through the same itinerary as before and did all the cooking for them. They

(From left) Anthony, Vita, Angela, and Luciana, Montelepre, Sicily, 2014.

had their very own personalized tour with me and although it was not the same itinerary as it is today, they loved every moment.

I'll never forget the look on Anthony's face when he tasted a *cannolo* in Tuscany and I told him, "Anthony, don't have a *cannolo* here. Wait until we go to Sicily!"

The Sicilians, who invented *cannoli*, know how to make them the best. The word itself comes from the Islamic Empire period in 9th-century Sicily and means "tube" in Arabic.

During our second leg of the tour, in Sicily, Anthony finally had that wonderful, delectable taste of a real Sicilian *cannolo* in Monreale, and it did not disappoint.

When I began scheduling tours, I assumed I would only be taking guests on these tours during my vacation times. But the following year, Angela referred me to one of her best clients, Mr. Sherman. He'd brought along his wife, Carolyn, and his sister and brother-in-law. It was about halfway through the tour that Mr. Sherman turned to me at breakfast and said, "This is the most relaxing and enjoyable vacation I've ever been on."

Shocked by this declaration, I thought, *how can this be?* These folks travel the world and have taken tours with some of the best tour companies. He and his brother-in-law are enthusiastic amateur photographers and take great pleasure producing slide shows of all the places they've traveled. Some of the best photos on my website are from Mr. Sherman's lens.

It then dawned on me what Mr. Sherman was saying. This tour spoke to his soul and how he was feeling about the experience of living in Tuscany for the week. It was not just about visiting tourist sites; it was about waking up each day in a countryside villa and visiting markets and wineries, then coming home each day to the aroma of dinner being prepared. Those days touched him and this convinced me that I could no longer wait until I retired ten years in the future to do this thing I was loving so much.

When I returned to my home in Florida, I decided I would quit my position at the bank and see if I could sustain myself by creating a full-time tour company. It was on my birthday in December that I sent in my letter of resignation. In 30 days, I would cease working for the bank and pursue a new business in the tourism industry.

That afternoon, at lunch hour, I went off to mail my application for a *Seller of Travel* license from the State of Florida. But as I drove down US 41, the envelope holding the application went flying out of the saddle bag of my motorcycle. You should have seen me rushing to turn back and search the side of the road. I must have looked like a madman to passers-by, but if you can believe it—I found it.

After retrieving the envelope from its roadside pummeling, I continued to my destination. At the Post Office, the clerk had a funny look on his face when he saw the tire marks stamped on the front of the envelope. *Was this an omen for what lay ahead?* I wondered. It *was* an omen all right, but it was a good omen, symbolizing how I would overcome any obstacles in my path.

As the days ticked by and we got into the holiday season, my assistant manager and I didn't understand why HR hadn't posted my position yet. I had my exit interview the week between Christmas and New Year's, and my final day was soon approaching.

Then, on Monday, January 5, the start of the first full week after the holidays, my boss called me to schedule a telephone meeting. Soon after we started the call, the company's HR representative in Dallas joined us and said that the bank had decided to close the office I was working in. She asked if I would be willing to continue past my January resignation date. She went on to say that "since the office is a deposit branch for the bank, the federal law requires a 90-day notice to its depositors before it can be closed."

Now, I cannot say I was completely surprised by the bank's decision. In the branch's 30-year history in Sarasota, it never got beyond managing the assets of its Michigan transplant clients who moved to Florida after retirement. Banking competition in Florida was far greater than any other market the bank operated in and after the recession our office would be the fourth in the state to close.

What did surprise me was the generous severance pay package they offered me and the three months of healthcare and a 20 percent annual salary bonus to stay on for the entire 90-day closure period.

This arrangement gave me a head start and some financial security to start my new tour business. Instead of relying on my savings to sustain me through the first few years, I would have a cushion to help me through the startup process.

As it turned out, I didn't need the cushion because my new venture was profitable from the beginning. I considered this a sign from above that I should follow my new career path. I had gone through such a difficult time during the recession, but somehow on the other end of it all, I was given this gift to help me justify the leap of faith it took to start a new career—indeed, a new life.

And further, I was truly blessed with the opportunity to rejoin the bank at the Sarasota office, because there couldn't have been a better place to market my new business. So many of our clients were transplants and snowbirds who flock there in retirement and are eager to travel. I had a direct line to my target market.

Looking back at the process of reinventing myself, I found it to be a lesson. I learned that so many of my life experiences had led me to find a career I'm passionate about. Everything I did in my prior employment helped prepare me in one way or another for the next step in my professional journey. The connections I had made throughout the years had also helped create a foundation for my new business.

I've never regretted walking through the proverbial door that my boss, Kurt, had opened for me in the summer of 2013. And though, as I write this book, the COVID-19 pandemic is still creating much uncertainty, I am sure that taking that leap of faith was the best decision of my life and I will forever be grateful to Kurt and Suzanne for inviting me on their Tuscany family vacation.

Chapter 2

THE CATALYST

O ver the past eight years, there has been a great deal of change in my life, and as I look back, I realize that the process of adjustment began to form even before the significant changes materialized.

I went from having a 24-year career predominantly in the banking and wealth management field to a boutique travel company at the age of 52. It was not a lifelong dream to create such a company. It just happened. Ultimately, it was born out of the desire to follow a passion for my Italian culture I had developed over the years. Then came the realization that such a passion could be shared with others who would be willing to pay for such an experience.

At the start of my new business, I lacked many qualifications that may have seemed like a requirement to start such a venture. I couldn't read or speak Italian; I had no experience traveling within the country by car, train or ferry. I also had little understanding of what authentic Italian cuisine was, outside of what I had read in books.

The fear of financial failure was present as well. Not to mention the people I care about and who care about me would sometimes, perhaps subconsciously, try to derail my dreams with things they would say. Early on, I was having a conversation with some dear friends when the husband said, "We have a longtime friend who's been in the travel business for many years, and she said that what you are doing won't work because . . . ."

The moment he said "won't work," I stopped listening. I wasn't going to let anything get in the way of what I believed in my heart and what I came to realize was my purpose. I had gotten a taste of what the experience could be and I was determined. I would not fail.

I may have had none of the qualifications on paper that would seem to suggest I could create a successful, high-quality tour business. However, I believed I had other qualities that made me uniquely suited for the job.

During that first trip to Italy back in 2012, when my son and I visited my grandfather's ancestral home of Montelepre, we were invited into the home of my cousins. That was a special moment because it gave me a true and authentic experience of everyday life in Italy. The emotional aspect of that time and my ability to recreate that experience for future guests was a key factor in my ability to succeed without having any of the qualifications I mentioned above.

In addition, without knowing it, almost everything I did in my career up to that point prepared me for my new job as a travel specialist. Because most of my first career was in the wealth management arena, I had a great deal of experience working with highly successful and sophisticated people. The level of service required to succeed for all those years also gave me an advantage. My former clients were the same demographic as the target market for my new business.

As it turned out, I was highly qualified to create a successful, premium tour-operator business after all. As I began to expand my contacts in Italy and make improvements to the overall experience, my tours became superior to even those offered by travel agencies. Plus, as an American with exposure to Italian culture (through my family and friends in Italy) I was able to create an authentic experience that was palatable to American tastes.

All of this centered on the passion I had for the culture and the food of Italy—the traditions I was born into.

Italian Cuisine

About five years before my first trip to Italy, I had begun to study the history of Italian cuisine. I was always on the lookout for books that could teach me the origins of the food. These weren't just cookbooks, but books about how these foods and dishes were shaped over thousands of years of Italian culinary history.

One book, *Italian Cuisine, A Cultural History*, by Alberto Capatti and Massimo Montanari, was very influential to me. It is a lush history of ingredients, dishes, techniques, and social customs behind the Italian food we know and love today. Another must-read to understand the regional aspect of Italian food is *The Food of Italy*, by Waverley Root. Root's adventures through the country document the vast array of cuisine, from Lombardy to Sicily, capturing the essence of the Italian table as well as its soul.

When I was living alone in Sarasota, I found myself longing for the days of my youth when Sunday dinner meant all the family coming together to enjoy a delicious meal. So, I decided to create my own Sunday dinner. I invited guests to crowd around my apartment table and eat the meals I had learned to prepare from my research and self-study.

Little did I know, it was practice for a time in the future when I would be performing many home dinner-theater experiences and "in-your-home cooking class dinners" for the hundreds of guests I've had the pleasure of entertaining since. These times were the beginning of the passion that was igniting within me, eventually resulting in my total reinvention.

Better Things on the Horizon

Is it possible that a simple, seemingly inconsequential decision can change your life in a monumental way? We all know that big decisions like whether to go to college, get married, or to have children create monumental changes in our lives. But who would have thought that deciding to go on a vacation could do the same?

After experiencing so much heartbreak and loss in the preceding years, I felt the pull to visit my grandfather Francesco Gaglio's hometown in Montelepre, Sicily. Maybe it was the curiosity of seeing firsthand where my grandfather lived and the kind of poverty and desperation that drove him to leave his home that drove me; whatever it was, I felt deep inside that visiting the place of my roots would put things in perspective. A much-needed perspective.

Although I'd suffered financial losses, my worthless company stock and options, and the devaluation of our home and investment assets, that was nothing compared to the absolute poverty my grandfather's family in Sicily had had to overcome.

The recession years were difficult, there is no doubt, but I was fortunate to have the position in Sarasota with the same bank I had been employed by for 16 years in Michigan. My income was less than before the recession, but I was tremendously grateful and more fortunate than most of my unemployed, banking-industry friends. And because the position provided a generous vacation benefit, I was able to take that first trip to Sicily, which seemed like the obvious choice. Something was pulling me to Montelepre, something that I was sure could heal me from the wounds of the past.

I asked my son, Anthony (Tony), who shares my love of travel, "Would you like to go to Italy with me and visit the little town where my grandfather was born?"

He quickly answered, "Yes!"

It was my first overseas trip, and I was excited to enjoy it with my son. Over half of my life had passed already, and I'd never ventured outside the northwestern hemisphere.

Robert Gaglio and his son, Anthony, at the Roman Forum.

Our adventure started in Rome. There we visited historic sites like the Colosseum, the Forum, and the Vatican. We also took a trip to Pompeii. One of the most enjoyable events was a bicycle tour through the city and into the Heights. In the evenings, we ate like kings (or should I say emperors), enjoying some of the most delectable food the city's restaurants had to offer.

After a few days in Rome, we started the second leg of our trip in Palermo. We were already exhausted as we disembarked at the airport. But we picked up a rental car and proceeded to drive into one of the craziest cities imaginable. Everywhere I looked there were cars zipping past, weaving in and out of oncoming traffic, and what seemed like an endless number of scooters buzzing all around our little rental car. Appropriately, Vespa means "wasp" in Italian. At one point my son turned to me and yelled, "Dad! Why are you driving so crazy?"

I answered quickly because after only 20 minutes of driving, I'd figured it out: "You either get hit or you hit someone else, and I'm not going to get hit!"

It was evident as we drove through the city that the economy was rough on Sicily as well. With its many vacant buildings and graffiti everywhere, it seemed clear it had taken a beating. But it had suffered and survived before.

In its 3,000-year existence, Palermo has taken on invaders and pillagers, and even been hit by Allied bombs during World War II. Some of those bomb scars can still be seen today. A world economic recession was nothing for this ancient city to handle, and I had the feeling it would go on for another 3,000 years.

We found our little hostel accommodations and settled in, and shortly befriended a British couple who was staying in an apartment near us. Because I love cooking for others and meeting new friends,

I invited them to join us for a meal I was planning for later in the week. I planned to cook a lavish meal with ingredients gathered from my grandfather's hometown. A culinary coming home of sorts.

After our hectic tour of Rome, our flight, and traveling through Palermo, we decided to spend a relaxing day at the beautiful beach of Mondello. But we soon found out that relaxing at the beach in Sicily was nothing like going to the beach in Florida.

It started with an endless search to find parking. When we finally did find a spot, a "parking man" demanded a euro—this is a kind of parking racket that exists in the South. Since it was a Saturday, the beach had already filled up with many other people looking to get a break from the heat, but we managed to find a spot that was just big enough to lay down our towels.

Once we settled in, we were barraged with an endless number of unofficial vendors hawking everything from cold beer and Coca-Cola to sunglasses. There was even a guy carrying a pole hung with sundresses.

A constant barrage of "*Birra*, Coca-Cola" inter-

Anthony at Mondello Beach, June 2012.

rupted our relaxation as the sweat poured down our faces. Then a skirmish broke out between two coconut vendors. Apparently, one of the men had been encroaching on the other's space and all hell broke loose. The two men were yelling at each other threateningly and coming close to blows. They had to be held back from each other by observers.

I'm sure much of the spectacle was for show, but it added to the sense of disorder of the day.

Now with all that going on, the temperature was climbing to around 105 degrees and the water wasn't much cooler. We had to take turns going swimming since what little we brought to the beach couldn't be left unattended.

As the sun reached its highest point of the day, we ate the lunch we had packed. Tony turned to me and said, "Dad, I'm melting."

We had been living in Florida for about seven years and were well accustomed to the heat. But this was well above the 92-degree average of a typical Florida summer day, and although the humidity was not as bad as in Florida, it was enough to make one's head swell.

Although visiting the beach that day was a colorful experience, I would not say it was a relaxing one. But Mondello is a beautiful beach town and in the years that followed, I learned the best way to experience a day at the beach was to stay at a hotel with a private one.

Since that first trip, I have chosen to stay at the Grand Hotel. It has been remodeled and has its own private beach. There are several restaurants as well, so it is a lovely place to enjoy the sunset and dinner. But I do recommend avoiding Sicily in the summertime if it's possible. Autumn is a much better time of year to experience it. It's much cooler so you can enjoy navigating the beautiful hilly towns and visiting historical sites, yet it's still warm enough to take a swim and enjoy the water.

With our beach day cut short, Tony and I had found ourselves with an extra half day to do something else. So going up the mountain where it was cooler to see if we could find some of our family members seemed like a good idea.

This was during the early days of Facebook, so I hadn't begun to use it yet, and of course, Ancestry.com had not been invented. Searching Sicilian hill towns for my cousins was more of an old-school process and we didn't know what to expect. We figured they were there, somewhere in the vicinity of Montelepre, since my parents had visited them in 1974, but we had no idea where. I had tried but was unsuccessful in contacting anyone before we left the U.S.

The city limits of Montelepre, Sicily.

Because my grandfather was now deceased, all we had with us was a piece of scratch paper that my father had prepared outlining what he knew of his Aunt Vita Gaglio-Cucchiara's family tree, on the back of a Valpak coupon—a list of scribbled names for whom we'd be on the lookout.

We drove our little Fiat 500 up the curvy roads until we reached the town of Montelepre, a town of fewer than 6,000 residents, (about 22) kilometers south of Palermo. The name translates to "hare mountain." As many times as I've been there though, I've

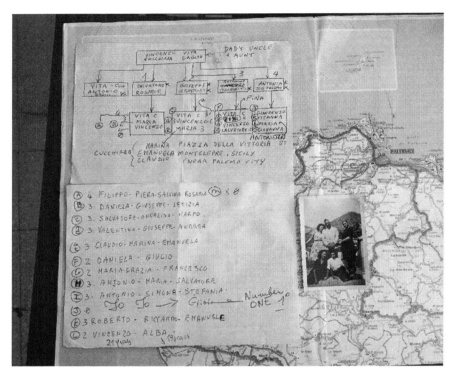

Aunt Vita's family tree written by my father with
a photo of my grandfather returning.

never actually seen a hare on the
mountain. I'm guessing they hang
out at night when it's cooler and
harder to be seen.

We rolled into the city less than
an hour later and were thankful
that we had such a small car. As we
climbed towards the center of town
every street seemed to get more and
more narrow. Approaching the city
center, a street sign reading "via S.

Via S. Gaglio, Montelepre, Italy.

Gaglio" stopped us dead in our tracks. I decided this was a good place to start searching.

I parked the car and we approached an elderly lady sitting on her front entry landing. It was barely a porch, but the shade from the adjacent homes and a breeze cutting through the narrow streets must have provided her some relief from the heat. I showed her my driver's license displaying my name, which matched the name of the street she lived on, and my dad's makeshift family tree. She looked at me with a curious smile and then called out for her daughter who quickly appeared. She grabbed her cell phone and said, "Cugina inglese," which I later learned means English cousin. She was calling a cousin of hers who could speak English.

I remember how blazing hot it was standing there in the street. After a couple of minutes had passed, a young lady with a ponytail walked up and said, "Hi, I'm Joanna La Perna from Windsor, Canada. They call me 'Americana' because I speak English, but I'm really Canadian."

"I'm from Detroit!" I told her. "We grew up just 40 miles apart. How did you end up here?"

She explained that after a year of college, she didn't want to return and decided to go on a vacation to spend time with family in Sicily. There she had met the man who would become her husband and decided to stay. That was 19 years ago. She now has two daughters and a happy life in Sicily.

I showed Joanna my scrap-paper family tree and explained that I was trying to find any of my father's relatives. I was a little reluctant because I didn't want to impose on her, but Joanna said, "I don't get to speak English much around here. I'm happy to help."

She examined the paper and explained that she may have known Giovanna Palermo (my father's second cousin) who she thought worked at her daughter's school. But she didn't know where she lived. So, we began visiting various businesses in town.

First, Joanna took us to a bakery to ask the owners if they knew anyone on the list. Then we hit a pizzeria called Pizze e Sfizi. The owner, Antonio Di Lorenzo, told us that Gianrenzo Palermo (Giovanna's brother) had just been there at 12:00 for lunch. We had our first lead!

We had a nice talk with Antonio who, as it turns out, had lived in Grand Rapids, Michigan, for about 15 years. He had brought his family back to settle in Montelepre.

Anthony Gaglio, Antonio Di Lorenzo, Robert M. Gaglio.

After a few more stops, Joanna had a good idea of where the cousin, Giovanna, may have lived. We soon found ourselves knocking on the door. An elderly, tiny lady answered and told us that Giovanna was at the beach and would return later that evening. We had found her! But we were at a momentary standstill. Joanna invited us to wait at her home.

On our way there, we stopped at a house where Joanna's husband, Filippo Licari, was working. He was there remodeling his cousin's home in town. It was very interesting viewing the reconstruction of a 300-year-old home. One thing is for sure: you make a lot of rubble when putting in new water and electrical lines.

Once at her house, Joanna served us cold Italian beer while we waited. I peppered her with questions about living in Sicily. We discussed food and how Sicilians prepare red sauce. She described the process from the beginning.

"It's a real hassle," she explained. "In the late summer, all the women put on gloves and swirl their fingers through crushed tomatoes on a big table outside. Once the tomatoes are reduced, they are placed in bottles for canning, to be used later."

To me it sounded like a way to make sun-dried tomato paste. At the time, I could only imagine the taste of the natural sugars brought out by the Sicilian sun. You'll never have better, I'll tell you that.

In Montelepre, each family also produces their own olive oil from their family olive trees. Joanna presented me with a liter Coke bottle containing the golden green oil and it felt like she was gifting me liquid gold. We sat and talked in her lovely remodeled home while her two daughters did their homework in the background. As Tony and I enjoyed our ice-cold beers, waiting for her husband to return, I was filled with excitement.

Gift of family olive oil from Joanna; Montelepre, June 2012.

Soon, Filippo came home. After taking a shower he took a look at the list and suggested that we go to the home where he thought Gianrenzo might live (Giovanna's brother).

We all packed into his car and a short ride later we pulled into a parking spot in front of Gianrenzo's home. He wasn't home, but we were received warmly by his family who welcomed us into the living room where we waited for Gianrenzo to return.

Just as we were enjoying a serving of gelato, Gianrenzo appeared. Joanna explained what was going on and handed him the family tree of his Great-Aunt Vita. I asked Joanna to explain that I didn't want to impose on him, but I was hoping to find my family members.

"Oh, that is not a problem at all," Joanna said. "He is very interested in meeting you, and he remembered when your parents visited them when he was a teenager."

Gianrenzo's eyes scanned the paper that listed the names of his aunts, uncles, and cousins. He soon picked up a pencil and began to make corrections. For the most part, however, my dad had done a fairly good job. He had a few of the in-law names wrong, and Gianrenzo marked off those who had passed. At that point, my father was 85 years old, so the likelihood of meeting any of his first cousins was slim. Out of the large group of Dad's first cousins, just two were still alive.

Mostly my dad's second cousins were living. As it turned out, my parents had stayed with Gianrenzo's family in Palermo that summer in 1974. What were the chances of meeting Joanna and her husband and having them lead me to one of the same cousins whose parents hosted mine on their one and only trip to Sicily 40 years prior? To me, it did not matter that they were second cousins of my father. I felt an immediate connection to these folks.

An excited buzz spread quickly through Gianrenzo's family. And as soon as Giovanna learned about the two Americans who had shown up at her doorstep while she was away at the beach, she asked Gianrenzo to bring us to her since she couldn't drive. Joanna explained to us that Giovanna had a defect from birth that had prevented her bones from forming properly. But despite her physical disability, she was the life of Montelepre.

Tony and I soon experienced her joyful energy firsthand when she greeted us at her door with her incredible smile. She was ecstatic to meet us and invited us in. As we sat around the kitchen table sipping our refreshments, Giovanna shared some of her many photo albums of our family. She also showed me a photo of my grandfather and explained many things about our family. As we visited, she became overjoyed and tears appeared in her eyes. It felt like a magical moment and I was awash with gratitude.

I will never forget the love that was in Giovanna's smile that day. It pulled me into my Sicilian family in an instant. These were the people my grandfather had left behind when he left for America nearly a hundred years earlier.

As the evening was waning, Giovanna invited us to stay for pizza with her aunt, Zia Vita, who was the little old lady we had met earlier in the day. By then Tony and I were physically and emotionally exhausted and had to decline the invitation. We asked if we could return the next day. Giovanna was happy with our proposal to return and invited us to join them for Sunday dinner that next day.

As we left, Giovanna and Zia escorted us to the street and showed us the home of my grandfather's family—directly across the street from her home. There sat a tiny, first-floor dwelling that had recently been turned into a garage with a brown door, but was once the home of seven of my grandfather's family members.

I was overwhelmed with emotion. A day that had begun with a failed attempt to relax at the beach turned out to be one of the most meaningful days of my life. In the years that followed, I realized some of my best days in Italy were the ones where I wandered about and just let the day unfold. You never know what the day might bring if you just let it.

First dinner in Sicily with my newfound family.

Tony and I climbed into our little Fiat to return to Palermo. He turned to me then and said, "Dad, I don't have the words to describe just how I'm feeling after what we experienced today."

He had taken the words right out of my thoughts.

I couldn't have known that my decision to take a vacation would transform my life, much like Joanna's life-changing decision to vacation in Montelepre had led her to meet her husband 19 years earlier.

Every day holds a new opportunity. You never know what life has in store for you.

The sun was already bright and warm by the time we got up the next morning and the excitement of spending the day with our new family was almost too much to bear. We had made arrangements to meet with Giovanna back at her home at 2:00 p.m. This also happened to be the day that I had planned to make dinner for Tony and a few British travelers we'd befriended along our journey. We were up for the cooking challenge and decided to find a market to pick up supplies before meeting Giovanna.

Just as we entered Montelepre, we found a little market. I gathered tomatoes, basil and other items for sauce, and I would use the olive oil Joanna gave me the previous day. To simplify, I picked out some ready-prepared *spiedini* from the butcher case. *Spiedini* was always one of my dad's favorite dishes that my mom would prepare. *Spiedini alla Siciliana* are grilled *scaloppine* (Sicilian-style veal rolls) that are stuffed with a mixture of breadcrumbs, cheese, pine nuts, raisins, and salt and pepper. The rolls are threaded on a skewer with bay leaves and onion slices between the meat rolls. They are grilled or broiled until brown on all sides. Later, I discovered there are many different kinds, though, with different combinations of stuffing. My cousin, Maria, makes *spiedini* with chicken, which is one of my favorites.

I learned quickly that in a little store like this you don't touch the produce. A man stands at attention ready to gather the items you want and places them in a bag marked with the price.

I'll never forget the smell of that store. It triggered a childhood flashback of visiting a store in the Bronx while on a trip to see my mother's family. Back then, 45 years earlier, that part of the Bronx was almost all Sicilians. The smell of that store in Montelepre was like a time machine taking me back to my 7-year-old self with all the colors and textures and smells so unique to Sicily and Sicilian cuisine.

Our next stop was Giovanna's house. Before we headed farther up the mountain to our cousin Vita's country home for our Sunday dinner, Giovanna and her sister, Vitanna, took Tony and me to the cemetery, or *cimitero* in Italian. Following that initial Italy trip, it became one of the first Italian words I remembered because every time we drove past the *cimitero*, my cousins would make the Catholic sign of the cross as a prayer. It just stuck with me.

Giovanna and Vitanna escorted us to the family gravesites that were contained in various mausoleums. Giovanna retrieved the keys from the attendant and opened the door of my great-grandmother Antonina Monacó's tomb. There etched in stone was her name, photograph, and the dates of her birth and death. This was the woman who tied us all together, our shared great-grandmother. She was the mother of Giovanna and Vitanna's grandmother, Vita Gaglio-Cucchiara, and the mother of my grandfather, Francesco Gaglio. In that moment I could feel the inherent love these cousins had for my son and me, and I knew for sure that I would return to Sicily again very soon to keep our connection going.

While at Vita's tomb, I noticed a parade of people going to one particular grave. Despite our language difficulties, I asked my cousin, "Why are there so many people going to that grave?"

She told me that it was the grave of the "Great Bandito," Salvatore Giuliano, who is still revered by the Sicilian people. This spot was like Graceland; people from all over Sicily came to pay their respects to the man known as the modern-day "Sicilian Robin Hood." Born and raised in Montelepre, Giuliano had dreamed throughout the war, and until his death in 1950, of making Sicily an independent country for the first time in its history.

That's a story for another day, but if you want to learn more, check out the movie *Salvatore Giuliano* by director Francesco Rosi. This 1962 portrayal of the Giuliano story depicts the complicated twists and connections between governmental and police powers, the Independent party, and the Mafia in 1940s Sicily. It's a great film.

It was on a later visit that my cousin Riccardo downloaded the movie on my laptop and explained to me that it was one of the first films to utilize flashbacks in a story. I can't confirm that fact, but I can say the movie's neo-realist style makes it well ahead of its time. In the trial scene that follows the death of Giuliano, there is a defendant with the name "Gaglio," which I got a kick out of. There were good odds that a Gaglio was in the Giuliano gang, since so many Gaglios can be found in Montelepre. In fact, about a third of the residents of Montelepre are Gaglios—which vastly improved our odds of finding them in the first place!

After the cemetery visit, it was time to head farther up the mountain, into the countryside, to a place called Calcerame, where Cousin Vita and her husband, Pino, have their country home. Vita is another cousin from my Great-Aunt Vita's family.

In southern Italy and especially in Sicily, families often have a second home higher up the mountain to spend summers growing produce and maintaining the olive trees for the fall harvest. The air is much cooler, and the nights give a great relief from the heat of the city. An already growing crowd of family members greeted Tony and me with hugs and kisses. Giovanna's friend Maria, who taught Italian at Auburn University in Alabama for 20-plus years before returning to Sicily, translated all communication between our Sicilian cousins and us strictly English-speaking American cousins.

We were greeted with warmth and instantly felt right at home. Pino gave me a tour of his vast garden with various vegetables, grapes, fruit and nut trees, out-of-this-world basil plants, other herbs, and of course, tomatoes. Hanging braided bulbs of garlic, figs, and tomatoes were drying out on racks, soaking up the sun. Inside, the women prepared the feast. My taste buds were already bouncing with anticipation.

We enjoyed a typical Italian menu. Homemade wine, meats, cheeses, nuts, and figs kicked off the meal as our antipasti. Next, we all sat at the kitchen table for the upcoming courses. Our first course (*primo piatto*) was a fresh homemade macaroni with a tomato sauce that exploded with flavor and was served with fresh ricotta cheese. Believe me when I tell you, you have never tasted ricotta cheese until you have tasted it in Italy.

The second course (*secondo piatto*) was a tasty, breaded chicken cutlet, sautéed veal, and a delicious fresh salad. They passed plenty of Sicilian bread—you know the kind, a hard crust covered with sesame seeds encasing a soft, spongy, white center. Then, we ate huge slices of ruby red, mouthwatering watermelon. It's a truly Sicilian custom to serve fruit after the meal and before the dessert.

Dolce (dessert) was an amazing experience because I got to participate in its making. The ladies had fun teaching me how to

Sfince di Prescia made with my cousins Vita and Maria.

make a tasty fried dough called *sfince di prescia*. This, combined with Sicilian gelato, ended the best meal experience I've ever had. Look for this recipe in the back of the book.

Evening was approaching fast and we still had another dinner to prepare for our British friends. That's right! We just consumed about 3,500 calories and then had to drive down the mountain to our apartment to prepare and consume another dinner. No problem!

During that second dinner, my cousin Luciana joined us for gelato. Our new British friends were clergy guides taking priests and ministers to the various sites, so they could help us communicate with Luciana. When we said goodbye, Luciana said, "The next time you come to Palermo, you stay with me in the home your parents stayed in when I was a child."

Luciana would become the link to my Montelepre family for years to come.

It was an incredible day, an experience that Tony and I will never forget. But the trip wasn't over. Our new family insisted we come back, so we agreed to return after a short tour of Sicily, plus a visit to Siracusa and Agrigento, both UNESCO World Heritage sites of significant Greek importance. After several subsequent visits to Siracusa, it has become one of my favorite cities in all of Italy.

We returned to Montelepre and were greeted to a royal welcome at a local restaurant. More than 30 guests treated us to—you guessed it—another multi-course meal. This time we were showered with gifts of wine and Sicilian mementoes as family members poured into the restaurant. It was a wonderful meal and Maria returned to translate our numerous conversations.

The husband of one of my cousins said something to me twice, at which point Maria turned her head and said, "Sicilian men repeat themselves a lot!"

Surprised, I said to Maria, "Oh my goodness, my ex-wife hated when I did that!"

I guess you really don't know who you are until you see where you come from!

Our adventures in Italy ended the following day. For me, that seemingly inconsequential decision to take a vacation changed my life forever. I was so moved by the experience of reconnecting with my family after generations apart that I made the pledge to return for as many years as possible to rebuild our family relations.

My tour business came to be because of me wanting to get to know my family more intimately, and the tours I have created over the past eight years are based on the emotions and feelings I experienced on that first encounter with the family my grandfather's sister and my Great-Aunt Vita had created. I've since introduced three of my four siblings to our cousins. I can honestly say I've experienced a great joy from the love I've received from my cousins over the past eight years and look forward to including them as family for the rest of my life.

Chapter 3

WHO'S IN CONTROL?

What gives a person the guts to take a giant leap and do something completely different from what they've known most of their adult life? In my case, it was a catastrophic turn of events.

The years from 2008 to 2012 were simply the worst four years of my life. It was during those few years that I lost a job for the first time in my professional career. I suffered great financial losses due to the collapse of the bank I worked for. Hell, even the stupid 529 college fund I invested in for my children in 1999 barely grew 2 percent over a 13-year period.

Financially, it was a disaster, but that was nothing compared to the emotional trauma of a family crisis and my divorce that finalized in 2012.

In May of 2010, I was fortunate to have landed a job with my former employer, Comerica Bank, in Sarasota. However, I was a physical and emotional wreck at that point. I weighed almost 220 pounds, despite the fact that I had been rowing with a rowing club about four days a week. The stress was inconceivable, and I can't imagine what I would have weighed if it hadn't been for that physical exercise.

I was depressed, had anxiety, and was extremely angry. I was angry over the way things turned out for me. I felt like I was just a bill payer and was tremendously lonely in a dysfunctional marriage. I felt the American Dream was a fallacy. After all the years of putting myself through college, working hard to build a professional career, dedicating myself as a husband and parent, and doing the responsible things like owning our own home and investing for the future, I felt like a man on a treadmill. I had run marathon after marathon but virtually gone nowhere.

But as I mentioned, along with the job in Sarasota came benefits and vacation time and I am forever grateful for both of those things. It was an incredible blessing to have the vacation time, but the medical benefits came in handy when I realized the crippling effects of my depression and sought professional help.

I remember the exact moment of my epiphany, following a period of just over two months in the winter of 2011 when I came home from work and just sat in front of the TV clicking through the channels in a never-ending cycle until about midnight. What was particularly odd about this phenomenon? Well, I was never the type to watch TV even as an adult. In fact, I went years without even having cable TV. During those gloomy nights, I sometimes watched some of the stupidest shows. Things like *1,000 Ways to Die,* which is about the stupid things people do that end up getting them killed. How crazy was that?

So, I found a therapist and went on medication to get better. I got my overweight body off the couch and joined the YMCA. I no longer had my rowing club nearby, so going to the gym and riding my bicycle was all I had to get exercise.

I lived in a beautiful city on the Gulf of Mexico, so in the evenings I rode my bicycle to the beach. Alone with my thoughts, I ate the dinner I had packed to enjoy as the sunset unfolded each night. Those nightly rides alone were a major help for me, but I will always be indebted to my therapist, Elaine, who helped me out of the deep hole I had found myself in.

As time went by, my anger and resentment turned into empathy and understanding. The pounds started falling off as I made a decision to forgo the daily insanity of mindlessly wasting my time and instead went to the gym. I took spin classes regularly and when that reached a plateau, I started taking weightlifting classes.

I wasn't embarrassed to be one of only a few guys in the class. I wasn't a typical gym-rat, carrying his gallon jug of water from machine to machine. I drew my motivation from our instructor, and the experience was a favorable reminder of my days when I belonged to a rowing club. Just like in rowing, where the coxswain calls out the rowing strokes, I needed to be told what to do by the class instructor. "Pick up that weight," and the calling out and counting of repetitions was what I needed to get motivated to do the work.

The combination of therapy, medication, and exercise began contributing to my emotional well-being. But I had turned my focus to the things I was eating as well. I put my cooking skills to work, eating only fresh food as often as possible. I laughed when I heard my son say, "Dad always has a lot of food in the house, but there is nothing to eat!"

My love of cooking was also healing me. Those foods needed to be prepared to make a meal, instead of pulling something prepackaged out of the freezer and blasting it in a microwave. In just a few years, I shed the 40 extra pounds I needed to lose to be healthy. And to keep reminding myself of how that excess weight felt, I always ended my workout with a jog around the YMCA with a 20-pound dumbbell in each hand.

Shame

One day, I was listening to a podcast called *Snap Judgment,* and this episode had a segment called "Shame." The producers of the show highlighted another podcast that was the brainchild of artist and interventionist Paula Williams. The Shamebooth is a traveling art installation, hotline, and podcast featuring the voices of real people sharing their shame.

The following excerpt from the podcast website describes the Shamebooth experience:

"You pick up the receiver and a voice welcomes you to share your story of shame, and you do. You are recorded with your consent, and in the act of speaking your shame and letting it go out in the world, you, hopefully, become liberated from that which holds you back."

As I listened to the Shamebooth stories, I started to think about what I would say if given the opportunity to give a confession about the shame inside of me. After giving it much thought, I realized that I had a great deal of shame in my life too. In fact, I realized that I had the shame of failure in almost every aspect of my life: as a professional, a father, a husband, and a person. In an attempt to unpack those feelings of shame, I decided to dig deeper (instead of ignoring it like I might have done only a few years earlier). This was a scary process, and even after all the years of trying to better myself, after all the therapy, I realized that I still had a lot of work to do.

As it turned out, the failures that occurred during the first half of my life would give me the courage to make changes in the second half. Perhaps it was failure that allowed me to let go of the person I *thought* I needed to be and I was no longer afraid of what I might lose. I was ready to take the leap of faith and create a new career that would allow me to follow my passion for travel and my Italian heritage. I was ready to completely reinvent myself. But, if anything about me was absolutely resolute, it was that I would not fail. Not again.

Looking back at the events that led to my shame, I now see why I was so driven to be successful in my new career. I finally learned to surrender to the fact that I alone have control over my emotions and how I react to the things around me.

My First Career

Now, when I say that I failed as a professional, I don't mean I wasn't successful overall with my banking career. I mean to say that there were different periods throughout my career where I let my personal problems and unhappiness interfere with my professional development. And that's much worse—the consequences are dire. It seems I could never come to a place where my professional career and personal life were successful and happy at the same time.

I had followed a career in banking, not because it was something I was passionate about but because it was stable, and for a long time I did enjoy it, especially as I advanced in my profession.

In high school, I had been an average student. But in my senior year, I had to decide what I was going to do. I wasn't very good at working with my hands and really didn't have an interest in being a tradesman of any sort. However, I was pretty good with numbers. I was the youngest of five siblings, and at that point my sister Roseann was the only one to go to college for a degree.

Like her, I had to figure out college on my own. My parents never attended college, let alone received a degree. At 18 years old, I needed to decide not only what I wanted to do with my life, but also figure out how I was going to pay for college on my own.

I ended up taking a year to figure it out, while still taking a few classes at the local community college. We called it "Twelve-Mile High" because of the road it was located on. My thinking was that if I didn't at least stay in some school while I was figuring this all out, I might not ever go back.

I spent the following four years learning to be a good student. Since I was paying the tuition and working as much as possible to get to the finish line, I had to do well. I was so fortunate to have the ability to take out student loans and deciding on a business degree in finance turned out to be greatly beneficial for me after graduation.

The summer before I left for Central Michigan University, I started dating Mary. Not only was I attracted to her great beauty, but she was one of the most loving and kindest people I had ever met. She seemed to be the perfect woman to build my American Dream with. I had a vision for what success looked like and she was right there with me. Together, we navigated and conquered the uncertain times as I worked to get through college. We married just a few years after I graduated.

I landed a job in credit with Comerica, which had a great credit training program. As I became a junior lender, I found it easy to succeed because I had such a strong work ethic, an easy way with people, and of course, I was very motivated. I remember being surprised when clients were grateful to me for having gotten back to them so quickly and couldn't understand why any other bankers wouldn't do the same.

After accelerating in the credit department, I moved on to wealth management sales—where I really excelled. It was there that I learned to listen to clients and understand their needs, providing a level of service far exceeding their expectations. The financial rewards were exceptional, but the industry was changing, and this style of wealth management was losing ground to Wall Street.

Looking back, perhaps I was ashamed of the fact that I never pursued a career as a Certified Financial Planner or went on to get my MBA. But I exceeded in sales. I didn't need an MBA to be a hunter. In the corporate world, to succeed, you either do the things you need to do to climb the ladder—like advancing your education or building connections and networks with those above you—or you work in sales and hope you don't burn out by the end of your career. Since I went the sales route, I eventually found myself in burnout mode. After two stock market crashes, endless banking and bureaucratic regulations after 9/11, and the recession of 2008–2010, I felt stuck. My burnout started to creep into my personal life and I realized that I needed to make a change, but I didn't know how.

Parenthood

The early days of parenthood were fun, albeit difficult, having two kids only 15 months apart. We had a traditional situation with Mary working part-time while a nanny watched the children.

Both Mary and I tried to make our kids' childhoods special, but she was especially good at it. She went all out when it came to celebrating everything from Halloween through New Year's Day. She took such care in making each holiday extraordinary. I remember one year hosting more than 160 guests for our annual

Halloween party. Mary went to great lengths to deck out the house with decorations, a bounce castle, and even a haunted house in the basement. But Christmas was her specialty. Each year she found the largest tree that could fit in our home and decorated the house from top to bottom. In our home, the incredible aroma of her baking was a true sign that Christmas was coming.

I, on the other hand, oversaw the recreational fun department. We loved to take the kids camping each summer in our RV, culminating every August with a three-week stay on Crystal Lake. Mary and I used to drive them up, get the RV and boat out of storage, and set up camp for the month. We spent hours boating, enjoying campfires, exploring the surrounding area's lakefront towns, and viewing amazing places like the Sleeping Bear National Shoreline.

A town in Benzie County even had a drive-in theater, the Cherry Bowl, which is still operating there today. The campground also had cable TV, which for kids who lived in a house without it was a dream come true. I remember them videotaping episodes of their favorite Cartoon Network shows to watch when they returned home.

There was so much more that went into raising our kids and I am proud of the job Mary and I did.

A Dark Turn

As it turns out, there were things beyond our control and I still feel shame for not being a better support to our daughter when things became exceedingly difficult for her. I didn't know it at the time, but what I saw as teenage angst and rebellion was actually the beginning of her mental illness. As her behavior became more and more erratic, I became angrier and angrier. I didn't understand what we had done wrong and why she was so hell-bent on making everyone around her miserable.

Eventually, we sought help from medical professionals, but the system didn't help much either. Most mental therapies weren't covered, and the selection of providers was limited since dealing with minors was difficult and the medications were more dangerous for them. In fact, I think the help we did get actually made things worse. There was one Harvard-degreed psychiatrist who spent very little time with my daughter before prescribing a powerful drug. We learned later that she had misdiagnosed her and the drug had no effect in dealing with her actual condition. There were other crazy things that led us to seek out another professional. But we never seemed to get actual answers—just more missteps and pain and confusion.

I became consumed with resentment and anger and my behavior was just as toxic. Our entire family unit was sinking into a dark place. We were all searching for a life raft and I should have been a better captain. Looking back, I am filled with unspeakable shame. Why couldn't I have done better? But the truth is, I couldn't have done better, I know that now. I didn't have the tools or the capacity. I was a completely broken man and I hope someday she can forgive me for all my inadequacies.

I always tell young couples planning to have children, "Parenthood is anywhere between hell and Christmas on any given day, and sometimes it is hell on Christmas."

Marriage

Is it possible to ever get over the shame of hurting the person you love? Here, too, I let anger, bitterness, and resentment consume my life, leaving little room for empathy and understanding.

I'm always amazed to hear divorced men (and women) speak ill of their ex-spouses. I think to myself *If she was that bad, what does that say about you? You married her!*

I don't blame my ex-wife for our failure. I fell far short of providing the commitment and trust my wife deserved. I let that anger, bitterness, and resentment take control of my emotions, resulting in pain and hurt for both of us. I failed at the most sacred personal relationship of all.

The Lesson

I've spent a lot of time reflecting on the path that led me to, what felt like at the time, utter failure. It was the realization that I could not have controlled the events around me that finally let me move forward and start regaining joy in my life. Since I had already been to hell and back, I didn't fear failure anymore. How much worse could it get? This time, since the children were adults and Mary was living a happy life without me, I was only responsible for myself. I made a personal vow that the next 40 years would be what I wanted them to be. I would follow my dreams and my passions.

I promised myself I wasn't going to be a "Willie Loman" character desperately chasing the "American Dream" but never achieving it. Instead of just dreaming about the things I wanted to do with my time in the future, I started doing them *now*. But make no mistake, I didn't do it alone. I opened myself to people I wanted to emulate and could learn from, and figured out how I could provide something mutually beneficial in return. My professional contacts, friends, and extended Italian family offered the means to achieve a deliberately chosen life. At the same time, my reinvented life has led to some of the best personal relationships I have ever experienced.

Chapter 4

ONE OF MILLIONS

According to Charles A. Wills, author of *Destination America*, more than 4 million Italians immigrated to the United States between 1880 and 1924, half of them between 1900 and 1910. The majority of these newcomers were fleeing harsh rural poverty in Southern Italy and Sicily. Both sets of my grandparents were part of that immigration story.

My maternal grandfather, Nunzio Mannino, worked and lived in New York alone for about 11 years before finally reuniting in Sicily with my grandmother, Rosa Gazzara, his three other children, and the rest of his extended family. I imagine the First World War had something to do with the long separation as well as the lack of resources. Whatever the cause that created the separation, he was able to return and continued to have children with Rosa, including my mother, Carmela.

My mother was born in Gualtieri Sicaminò, Sicily in October 1925. She immigrated with her family to the U.S. through Ellis Island in 1927. I found it interesting that she had older siblings who were born in the U.S., yet being younger, she had been born in Sicily.

My mother, Carmela (about age 24), circa 1949, The Bronx.

My mother's parents had traveled back and forth to America before they settled for good in the Bronx, New York. I later came to understand that it was common for people to go back and forth before finally choosing to either resettle, or remain in their home country.

The ship Carmela Mannino Gaglio and her family traveled on, called the Conte Biancamano in 1927.

The passenger list showing Carmela Mannino-Gaglio's
family arriving in New York City, June 15, 1927.

The Library of Congress reports that within five years, between 30 and 50 percent of this generation of immigrants would return home to Italy, where they were known as *ritornati* (returned).

I'm fortunate my mother's family decided to settle in the Bronx, where my mother lived until moving to Detroit after my oldest sister, Frances, was born. As a result of their migration, and growing up in the United States, I had the opportunity to pursue higher education and have a reputable career, which would have been harder to achieve in Sicily.

Living in Little Italy, the Bronx, would have been in some ways remarkably familiar for my grandparents. So many of the immigrants there were Sicilian, and they may have even known some of their neighbors from back home. The food, the customs, and culture would have been recognizable.

The two things that would have seemed very unfamiliar, though, would have been their access to an abundance of food and higher standards in housing in the U.S. Although apartments were still small quarters, they had indoor plumbing and much better living conditions than in Italy. The fact is, in parts of Sicily and southern Italy, there were still people living in cave structures with facades constructed on the outside of the cave. You can still see evidence of these abandoned dwellings throughout southern Italy, especially in Sicily.

My father's parents were from that small town in Sicily I've already told you so much about. Montelepre was the place my grandfather, Francesco Gaglio, left in 1912 at the age of 18 along with his cousin, who was also named Francesco Gaglio. Like many others, they came through Ellis Island. There were two others from their hometown who were also on that boat heading to Detroit.

They sailed on the SS Taormina from Naples, en route to New York. This transatlantic ocean liner was built and launched in Scotland in 1907 for an Italian shipping line. The Taormina was briefly chartered as a troopship for the US Armed Forces in 1918 and was eventually scrapped in 1929.

Documents state that my grandfather was a year younger than his cousin Francesco, who was described as having a scar on his nose, and was illiterate. My grandfather was going to see his uncle Salvatore in Newark, New Jersey, and Francesco was on his way to visit his cousin Luigi at the same address. It was also noted that my grandfather and Francesco were headed to Little Falls, New York.

The Little Falls Historical Society Museum has an article on their website about the Little Falls Textile Mill and the Phoenix Knitting Mill strikes of 1912, when there was much unrest because of unsafe working conditions and low wages paid to workers in the factories. Most of the striking workers were recent immigrants from southern and eastern European countries, principally Italians, Poles, Slovenians, Slovaks, and Czechs who lived on the south side of Little Falls in densely crowded tenement apartment houses. It's impossible to know now, but I'd wager the two cousins were on their way there to find work in the mills.

Documents also listed the two as "*campagnuolo*" or field workers. My grandfather had $20 in his pocket, paid his own fare, and was asked if he was an anarchist, to which he answered, "No."

He went on to spend two years in Rochester, New York, and then moved to Detroit where other former countrymen from Montelepre lived.

In Detroit, he worked on an assembly line for the Cadillac Motor Company, which by then was already established as an automaker known for precision engineering and stylish luxury finishes. Its cars were ranked among the finest in the United States.

Eventually, grandfather opened a market on Mack Avenue in Detroit. It was the 1930s and although Prohibition was repealed in 1933, you still needed permits and government permission to produce the alcohol. However, this didn't seem to stop my grandfather from making spirits. A story told by my father placed his then ten-year-old self hiding behind a garage with my grandfather while the police broke up their illegal still.

In 1924 Francesco married my grandmother, Francesca. She was 17 years old; 13 years younger than my grandfather. My father, Joseph, was born the following year. My aunt Antoinette was next, and then several years later, my Uncle Gus was born in 1935.

Unfortunately, I don't know a lot about my grandmother. It's a sad story, because after Gus was born, she began to suffer from mental illness. She most likely suffered from depression, and possibly had bipolar disorder. My uncle Gus was a young boy when she ultimately ended up in a mental institution during the last five years of her life. Her death certificate documents that she died on September 1, 1944, less than a month from her 36th birthday in the Ypsilanti State Hospital. The immediate cause of death was pulmonary tuberculosis, which she suffered from for ten months. Other "contributory causes of importance" listed "insanity, duration unknown."

I remember my father telling me about getting a leave from the Navy to visit her just before she died. It wasn't a pleasant experience for him and he didn't speak a lot about her.

My father went back to the Navy base and ended up in Japan after the war ended. My uncle Gus's remaining childhood was motherless. He was instead taken care of by various family members and ended up living with my aunt, who was then a young bride living in Grand Rapids, Michigan.

Dad's (Joe) Navy photo, circa 1942, Hawaii.

Above: Grandpa's shop in Detroit, Michigan, circa 1930s.
Below: Dad's shop in Grosse Pointe Woods, Michigan, circa 1960s.

My grandfather went on to have various businesses, one being a record shop called Toni's Records at 9100 Mack Avenue in Detroit. He had named it after my aunt Antoinette. The site is currently a vacant lot, but back then it sold Decca Records. Which is maybe why my father played piano and had a passion for music. He too sold records in the 1950s, '60s and early '70s on Mack Avenue, but in Grosse Pointe Woods.

My father had gone to school to learn electronics in New York after his discharge from the Navy. It was there in the Bronx where he met my mother at a wedding.

After my sister Frances was born, they decided to move to Detroit, where the rest of my family was established. He opened a TV repair shop and sold records and some musical instruments in the front of the store. He always supplemented his income with gigs his band would perform at parties, weddings, and other events in the Detroit area.

Dad (Joe) playing piano with a cousin's daughter, New York, circa 1953.

My life transition is especially rooted in my grandfather Francesco's life, for it was my desire to visit his place of birth that set me on my journey. He established our lineage, which made it possible to pursue my own Italian citizenship. Thus, returning full circle.

My grandfather must have been brave as well as driven to leave Sicily at 18. Through the years he lived in New York, Detroit, then back in New York, before finally settling and spending the rest of his life in Ontario, California. It's possible

Dad (Joe) playing piano in his Navy band The Reefers, Hawaii, circa 1942.

that my desire to travel and move around comes from him, although that desire came much later in life for me. I found it interesting that my grandfather came to America in search of opportunity and it was in Italy that I found my opportunity exactly 100 years later.

I was returning to Italy to stop focusing on making money so I could follow my passion for travel, food, and Italian culture. Sharing this passion is the basis for my tour business, and the process of reinventing myself and creating this new career has forever enriched my life.

Chapter 5

BUILDING SOMETHING FROM NOTHING

One of the best things about starting a business from nothing so late in life is that it made me use my brain in different ways. Writing a business plan, figuring out the best way to market and promote, all the advertisements/blogs/social media postings, planning the logistics for my tours, and even taking Italian lessons all required me to alter my perspective. I'd had a career in sales, so I wasn't afraid to get out there and promote. Since I am so passionate about what I do, that part was easy. The hard part was figuring out how to best allocate my limited resources: time and money.

One of the first things I did after writing my business plan was build my first website. I was so fortunate to have a brilliant son, Anthony (Tony), who helped me create it. Because he is an amazing self-taught digital artist, he created the logo for my company—for which I have received many compliments over the years. I was so grateful to experience working with him, and Tony's contribution to the company in the beginning was vital to its success. The quality of that first website was so good, I shortly landed a client from Seattle who'd found me on the internet and booked a week-long tour for a group of ten. The pride I have for Tony's effort is immeasurable and working with him was fun and special for both of us. Tony is also my biggest fan and has always given me a great deal of encouragement throughout this process.

With the website live, I then plugged all the contacts I had into an email marketing service and broadcast the news of my career change. I did the same on Facebook and LinkedIn and even setup an Instagram presence.

I was pleasantly surprised by the reactions I received from people I would talk to about my touring business. Many people would even approach me when they saw my shirt logo and ask about it. This never happened to me in the banking business. There are over 150 banks in the State of Florida, and I was one of many in an industry that wasn't very interesting. But people's eyes lit up when I talked about how I'd created my tour business. They often told me that such an adventure was on their bucket list.

But I had to adjust my expectations after meeting so many people with this same reaction. Even though what I was doing was so desirable and so infectious and so many people told me that it was something they wanted to do, only a small number I met were possible clients. Still, it was refreshing to have so much interest in what I did after a long, way less interesting career in banking.

Because I was starting from nothing, I had to learn the most efficient ways to promote my business—and fast. I soon realized that the best way was face-to-face contact with people in my target market. What

I was offering appealed to a very niche market. The value proposition could only fully be explained in person, so there would be time to show the difference between my tour and a tour arranged by a travel agent. Plus, they would get a chance to see my enthusiasm and hear my unique story.

In my business plan, I had to come up with several ways I could meet people. Most of them turned out to be successful in their own ways. One of the first steps I took was to hold events in various specialty stores, like olive oil shops and gourmet markets, where I gave cooking demonstrations. Over the years I've developed many classes for lifelong learning schools which combine education, culture, food, and entertainment. This approach allowed the guests a multi-sensory experience so they could make a deeper connection.

These classes provided a great opportunity to meet people who were active and interested in other cultures and travel. It also allowed me a way to promote my business while earning a small amount of income to cover the cost of the promotions. So, I didn't have to pay for advertising, which I learned never worked anyway.

I taught at several schools in Sarasota and after a while I became known in the community as "the former-banker guy who has an Italian tour company now." These classes were fun for me and very enjoyable for the participants. We not only provided delicious food and interesting information, we also had a live performer singing opera as people enjoyed their meals.

I spent the first three years doing as many of these types of events as possible. I held cooking demonstrations at the farmers' markets, along with a kids' pasta-making day, and silent and live auctions for charity events. I have no idea if the exposure helped in marketing my tour business, but I had a blast doing it.

An Italian dinner event at the center on Anna Maria Island.

Caponata antipasto for home dinner theater.

One of my favorite auction items was a dinner I'd developed based on the book *How Italian Food Conquered the World* by John Mariani. The idea came to me while listening to a radio interview with the author. That's how I decided to create a multi-course dinner that follows the themes from the book and also have an opera singer perform in between each course.

We've performed the *"How Italian Food Conquered the World"*-themed dinner many times since. It's been sold at various charity auctions for over $7,000 per event and has raised over $40,000 since we began. The winning bidder gets to make their kitchen and dining room the stage as we prepare a seven-course meal for them and their guests. I can't tell you how many guests tell us at the end

Robert cooking at a home dinner
theater event.

of these dinners that they have never experienced such an enjoyable feast. We've even had many people so intrigued by the concept that they've hired us for special celebrations.

My goal was to create an experience that our guests would remember for years to come. And that is just what I did.

As I said earlier, I couldn't have succeeded at this if it weren't for a few special people in my life who worked with me through the years. Joy Leitner, a wonderful singer, has delighted many of our guests for these dinners as well as at the many classes we provided

Serving crew for the "How Italian Food Conquered the World" home dinner theather; left to right: Roseann Gaglio, Cheryl Yeats, and Lisa Yellen.

at the lifelong learning schools. Cheryl Yeats started as a server for me and became an assistant chef and now travels to Tuscany with me to be the morning chef and house manager for our guests at the villa. Catie Briggs, a friend I made shortly after moving to Sarasota in 2010, has been working with me from the very beginning. With her by my side, I had all the confidence I needed to launch this new endeavor. She has worked so many events, dinners, and classes and she is my biggest promoter. These people, as well as others, were placed in my life and helped pave my path to success and I'm forever grateful for them.

In those early days, I had worked with a new, local food tour company, Key Culinary Tours. They provide food tours for locals and vacationers. Although it had been many years since I worked for tips, I enjoyed meeting all our guests and it was a great way for me to promote my new business. Spending hours with eight or more guests telling stories and guiding them to delicious local restaurants was a great way to get to know them and share my story.

The timing of this work was also perfect since the high season for southwest Florida is winter, which is the off-season for visiting Italy. The Sarasota area is filled with residents and snowbirds alike, looking to get away from the northern cold and for things to do. And then when the weather gets hot and uncomfortable, they look to travel north or take vacations until it is cool enough to return to Florida.

As I traveled through Italy, I've spent much time studying Italian cooking, taking cooking classes in Bologna, Florence, and Catania, and working to improve my skills as an Italian chef. After six years of preparing Tuscan barbecue, I finally became a master of the Tuscan cookout, grilling the famous *Bistecca alla Fiorentina* for our guests.

This is a four-inch beef T-bone steak cooked five minutes on each side and five minutes standing on its cross bone.

For me it's like a ritual: I take our guests to the butcher, where he chops the steak in front of us. I prepare the grill with real charcoal that has recognizable grains of the wood it comes from, not the chemical-filled, pressed charcoal that looks distinctly artificial. I cook the steak to perfection with fresh rosemary, salt, and olive oil. Finally, I carve it for our guests to enjoy along with my favorite *rosticciana*. These ribs are so delicious you only need a little salt and pepper. No sauce required!

Of course, collecting emails, writing newsletters, blogging, and constantly looking for ways to promote my tours was a full-time job. Although from afar, looking at my Facebook posts, it seemed like I was living the high life traveling in Italy (and I was), I was also working extremely hard and looking for clients any way I could. All that new activity was helping me grow and learn new things.

As the years passed, I learned that I was presenting to the travel market the very thing that the market was looking for. This is why Airbnb started offering experiences along with accommodation listings on their platform. I hadn't known this when I began this process, but as I became more entrenched in the travel industry, I learned that travelers today want more of a cultural experience. I just happened to get that right when I created a tour based on my own emotional connection to travel.

I remember working so hard in 2017, but it wasn't a very good year, with just a few tours booked. However, by the end of 2017, I had already booked three tours for 2018. I realized that my sales process ranged from eight to 18 months. So instead of getting discouraged, I worked even harder, realizing that the benefits would come. It just takes a little longer because people tend to plan this type of tour over a long period. Sure enough, the following year turned into a great year, with six tours in Tuscany, a tour in Sicily, and several private tours.

All of this created a multitude of connections, each providing opportunities to meet more people and create more sales. I wish I could say doing any one activity would provide me with all the bookings I would need to be successful, but that's not the case. There is no silver bullet to make things happen. It just takes a lot of effort to be seen and heard, and then maybe an opportunity will come.

I remember setting up a three-part series one season for an art center on Longboat Key that was operated by Ringling College of Art + Design. Unfortunately, the classes were scheduled for March, and just before they were to start, the school sent out an email explaining the Longboat Key Art Center would close in May.

Although I was still able to do the classes, many of the students assumed the place was closed and very few people participated. There I was loading and unpacking my cooking supplies, presenting, and breaking everything down each week with very few guests attending. But then on the last day of class, a couple, Christine and Ed, walked into the art center before going to get lunch at a nearby restaurant. The person working the front desk persuaded them to stay for the class, which brought the total attendance to seven. After class, Christine stayed to look through my picture book of the Tuscany tour.

"This is exactly what we want to do for our 50th anniversary with our family," she told me. We talked about it, but they soon left for home. Then, as I was loading my car with my traveling cooking show, I received a text from the couple stating that they had looked at my website and wanted to schedule a meeting with me the following Monday.

When I showed up and started to tell the couple about our tour, Christine stopped me and said, "Oh Robert, you don't have to sell us on the tour; I just want to tell you all about our family."

It turned out that they booked a tour in Tuscany for their entire family so that they could all celebrate their anniversary, which meant a customized tour for ten people. That experience in Tuscany was exciting for me because I had never designed a more personal tour. Having just the one family and children being involved made it that much more memorable. They were wonderful people, and the young grandchildren were delightful to have at the villa. Not having had children on my tours before, I bought some toys for the yard and pool as well as a soccer ball. I placed small Lego sets on their dinner plates to make them happy to come to dinner. Seeing the love this family had to share was one of the most amazing tour experiences I've ever had. I became very close to the family after that, seeing them in the winters and even visiting them several times at their home in Chicago.

That experience taught me that no matter how small the audience for my demonstrations, it could turn into something big. Not only was it a fruitful business opportunity, but I had gained dear friends in the process. So now, I never get disappointed when I have a small audience. I just go forward with all the passion and enthusiasm that I have for doing what I love most.

In only a few years, I went from a discouraged and unsatisfied professional in the business world to feeling like the motivated young man I was 25 years earlier. And I was completely enjoying my new career. Building something from nothing was exactly what I needed at that point in my life, and it just so happens that I found something to build that fits me perfectly. Undeniably.

Chapter 6

FREEDOM TO WANDER

One of the most rewarding aspects of my professional transition has been the freedom to control my time. Once I was released from the time structure of the corporate world, I had the freedom to allocate my time to the things that were most important to me. And I dedicated my schedule to building on this new dream of travel.

When you think about it, time is the only thing we truly own. We have complete control over how we spend our time, and it is up to us to make that decision. We own this decision. Therefore, we truly own the time that God has given us. Material things will come and go. The expensive vase could shatter on the floor, that new car could be totaled in an accident, a high-end computer could be damaged after only a year of use. Although objects can bring us happiness, they can never put us in a state of joy. Once our time has all been used, we'll have passed from this life on earth.

And who knows how much time we have. Our time on this earth could be long like it was for my parents—they both lived into their 90s—or it can be short like it was for my grandmother, Francesca Spadafora Gaglio, who died just before her 36th birthday.

In my former way of life, my goal was to build a massive retirement war chest. I would use it when I retired in my late 60s, to travel and do all the things I had dreamed of when the time finally came. In the past, much of my time was allocated to work. Although it provided a great deal of financial rewards and much satisfaction, I truly didn't own most of my time.

I had a generous vacation allotment and a good income to provide the discretionary funds to travel. But I was still limited in how I could use my time because I had committed to my career in the corporate world. Plus, my heart was no longer into what I was doing. The endless banking regulations that resulted from the 9/11 terrorism attack and the 2008–2010 financial crisis made me feel more like a governmental bureaucrat keeping track of clients instead of providing services to help them. These circumstances created an environment that was no longer fun and interesting. I saw the future written on the wall and before circumstances would inevitably change for me, like they did in the recession, I wanted to control the change for myself. Then came a reminder that life can be short and I needed to move on while I still could.

At the bank, there had been a senior manager based in Texas, whom I genuinely liked. Her office was in the bank's corporate headquarters in Dallas. The responsibility of the Florida bank's retail assets belonged to her and she visited us a few times during the period I worked there. She had such empathy for our situation since the asset size in Florida was a small allocation compared to the overall size of the bank. We were coming off a difficult recession and since the bank had little market share in the state, it was difficult to compete.

However, her visits suddenly stopped. This wasn't because she'd left the bank or was reassigned, but because she'd become ill with pancreatic cancer. She'd given a gallant effort battling cancer and trying to work from home but only 11 months later, she lost that battle.

Witnessing this wonderful, talented, and compassionate person die before her daughter's 20th birthday had a profound effect on me.

What good would it do if I played it safe and continued the corporate path, I wondered. The thought of having to relocate to another town to find work, only to spend the next 10 or 15 years in a profession that was no longer satisfying, sounded exhausting. It would only lead to time passing without doing the things I was passionate about. Plus, I had just watched a tremendously successful young woman die without coming close to reaching retirement. Yes, indeed, it was a sign.

At that point, I had already taken my first group to Tuscany and the idea of creating a tour company focused on a deep personal experience didn't seem too high-impact. In order to take the big step necessary, I had to change the way I understood the idea of compensation. For someone who spent the last 24 years measuring success on a monetary basis, this was not easy. The question "What is compensation?" had to be answered and understood before I could make the leap.

I had to rewire my brain to understand that compensation was not limited to the amount of money deposited into my bank account, but also includes a wider range of benefits associated with the work. There were several benefits I considered when determining that I wanted to create my tour business.

What I discovered was that having control of my own time didn't have monetary benefits, but ended up being priceless. I was able to use my time doing the things I had always wanted to do. It allowed me the freedom to meet new people, make new friends halfway across the world, connect with my Sicilian family, and even build deep, loving relationships with some of them.

Yes, my income took a deep cut and I no longer had the ability to max out my 401K contributions or take part in some of the things I enjoyed doing, like buying season tickets to the local theater, for example. But I wasn't working just to pay a large income tax bill every year either. And if those maxed-out 401K contributions were needed to allow me to travel when I retired, it didn't matter, because I was already traveling as a regular part of my new lifestyle.

At the time, my travel outside the U.S. was limited to the few trips I had made to Italy. But I wanted to travel extensively *now*, not just when I retired at some future date. Through my business I was creating an opportunity that would take me across the Atlantic to Europe every year. I could plan side trips by simply jumping on a plane or train to visit other countries before or after my work was completed. To me, this seemed like an invaluable benefit to my work that I hadn't considered before. As it turns out, I was immensely compensated! In recent years, I've never let the fear of scarcity get in the way of spending money on travel. I've looked at it as part of my new life and have been greatly rewarded for it.

Over the past eight years, I've been able to visit far more places than I could have ever visited in my old life, regardless of how generous my vacation time was. I've had the freedom to wander.

I've spent time exploring cities like Amsterdam, where I was moved by Van Gogh's work. I've visited the house Anne Frank's family hid in during WWII. I've taken a boat tour in Oslo, Norway, with breathtaking views of the fjord. I've experienced a train ride through the mountains from Paris to Milan that was like living in a beautiful model train set, passing picturesque towns with their buildings and homes adorned with snow. I fulfilled a lifelong desire by finally being able to walk the streets of Paris and enjoy the city's famous beauty and cuisine. I was able to wander through London, Nice, Barcelona, and the French Riviera. I'm no longer confined to the parameters of the weekends or vacation time to do what I want with my time. The ability to rent a car and travel the back roads in Tuscany going from town to town is such a simple pleasure—these are just a few of the "compensations" I have earned from my new career.

Assisi

Every year when I completed a tour season, I'd return through Detroit so I could visit my parents and taken advantage of the time we had together. And whenever I spoke to my mother about my latest trip, she always asked me, "Did you visit Assisi?"

I always replied, "No, Ma, not this year."

You see, for Catholics, Assisi is a pilgrimage location and kind of a spiritual Ground Zero of a great man who became a saint and dedicated his life to God's people. St. Francis had come from a wealthy family and could have had anything he wanted in life. Instead, he dedicated his life and vocation to helping others who had little or nothing.

I didn't quite understand the draw to Assisi that Catholics and others have had over the centuries, until the day in 2015 when I

Assisi, Italy (iStock photos).

finally visited. Assisi is located just south of the Tuscan border, two hours south of San Casciano, where we host our guests on our Tuscany Tours.

My girlfriend at the time, Frannie, and I had planned to visit a friend who rents a villa in Tuscany every year. Her little town is not far from Assisi, so Frannie suggested we visit the town where St. Francis (her namesake) lived during the 13th century.

When we arrived, we parked in a large parking garage cut into the rock and I thought, "Wow! There must be quite a few people coming here considering the size of these parking garages."

We started our adventure on foot and I realized just how many people came to see the town where St. Francis lived. In October, we were well past Italy's peak season and yet there were still thousands of people doing just what we were doing.

Standing on the top of a hill, viewing the Basilica of St. Francis, we could see a row of people waiting in line to enter. Dozens of people were seeking the opportunity to see and touch the tomb of St. Francis, located in the old church below the cathedral. We walked down the hill and through the town and when we reached the cathedral, a sensation came over me akin to the feeling I had seeing the Grand Canyon and Niagara Falls for the first time. It was surreal and moving, yet calming.

When it was our turn to enter the church, we stopped to visit one of the padres who was there taking requests for masses for loved ones. I thought of my mother. For several years, she had had this sense of hope for me to visit this beautiful place, which she experienced many years before. We made the arrangements for a mass for her and then continued to the basement. As we stood in line, with Frannie's hand in mine, a sense of peace and tranquility came over us.

As we walked back through town to find a little place for lunch, we were also looking for just the right gift to bring home for my mother. There was an old man working his craft as a jeweler in a little studio no bigger than a walk-in closet. Without speaking any English, he invited us in. There, we gazed at a variety of rosaries he had crafted. In his tiny creative nest, we searched for a fitting rosary to bring Mom. It was important that the rosary be crafted by a local artist. Then, I found it—a perfect rosary. It had simple earth tones, which for me symbolized the minimalism of St. Francis. I hoped it would bring that vibe to my mother that both Frannie and I had gotten from this beautiful place. I will forever be thankful for my mom's persistence to make sure I visited the place where St. Francis had lived. That visit to Assisi, the little town that my mother had asked if I had visited so many times, turned out to be one of my greatest experiences in all my travels through Italy.

Mother

One of the greatest gifts my new career afforded me was the ability to spend the last three weeks of my mother's life with her. I had just returned from my second tour season and my mother was very sick. But it was as if she had waited for me to return to the States.

Earlier that year, on a day when our Tuscan guests were out for their tour, I was back in the kitchen preparing for that night's dinner. It was a beautiful time in the villa; so quiet, and peaceful. I was enjoying being in the kitchen preparing food for our guests so much and thought it would be nice to FaceTime my parents. My mother answered and I propped my phone on the table. We talked for a while as I continued to work. It was like she was with me, in Tuscany, creating the day's meal for our guests, even though my parent's traveling days had long passed. Oh, how I would have loved to have them visit Italy with me, especially Assisi and Sicily! But today's technology provided the next best thing: a loving conversation with my mother.

I remember how worried I had been that year that something might happen to Mom while I was in the middle of a tour. Early that November, I had visited my parents for a week. One night before dinner, I gave Mom the rosary from Assisi. She smiled and began to cry. I can't help but believe she knew then that she would be leaving her family on earth and returning to that peaceful place called Assisi.

Although my mom had clearly declined since the last time I had seen her in early summer, she still sat at the dinner table and allowed me to serve them my home-cooked meals before she retired to bed.

Giving mom a rosary from Assisi, November 2015.

That visit affirmed for me that my mother's condition had greatly deteriorated. So, I made the time to return before Thanksgiving. Unfortunately, the meals that I had prepared during my previous visit would be the last time I would cook for her.

On Thanksgiving Day our family came to my parents' home. I had orchestrated the full traditional meal for my dad, brothers, sister, brother-in-law, nieces and nephews. We set up a makeshift dining room in the living room to be close to Mom's bedroom. We all took turns visiting her as she laid in her bed, too weak to come to the table, too weak to even eat. I remember my niece Carla saying, "I love you, Grandma!"

"I love you, too," Mom said, with all the energy she could muster. But even at that point, we didn't know that we were saying goodbye.

Someone from hospice visited the following day, so we could learn what was next and how we could help our mother. I was the one who would give Mom the morphine to help her with the pain. It was on a strip that melts on the tongue. After dinner, when I gave her the first dose, she sensed something was different with the medicine and with a clear eye said, "No junk!" She had earlier expressed that morphine "junk" was too strong and was not something she would need. But we didn't want to see our mother suffer any more than she had to.

I lied and said this was the way she had to take her medicine now. That night, I dragged a little mattress into her room and slept on the floor beside her hospital bed. I couldn't sleep so I sang to her as she slept. Around 4:00 a.m. her breathing became ragged and I could tell she was having difficulty. I had forgotten that the hospice nurse said that just before death, breathing becomes difficult. Mom was in such discomfort and I felt helpless trying to soothe her. I brought her water and moved up the back of the hospital bed so she could drink. I knew she was totally conscious because she moved her hand to signal for me to stop raising or lowering the bed.

I was frightened to see her in so much discomfort and I gave her another dose of morphine. She soon fell back asleep, and although I lied to my mother about the morphine, I felt justified seeing her sleep so comfortably. It was probably the best sleep she had had in several days. I struggled to sleep the rest of that night and when I finally did a few hours later, I woke to total silence in the room and I knew. Mom had passed, no doubt hand in hand with St. Francis.

My sister, Frances, suggested I place that rosary I'd bought her in Assisi in Mom's hands for her funeral. Afterwards, she recommended I take it away with me. When I returned to the villa in Tuscany the following year, I placed the rosary just above the light switch by the door of the kitchen. Although Mom was no longer there for me to FaceTime with, she *was* there! Each morning when I reached for the light to make the morning coffee, and each night after the staff finished serving our guests, as I turned off the light and retired for the night, Mom was with me.

The connection I had with my mother's cooking is what helped me heal from the loss. One of the fondest memories I have from childhood is dipping the fresh Sicilian bread my father picked up from the bakery after Sunday mass into the pot of meat sauce my mother prepared in the morning while we were still sleeping. The combination of the crunchy bread crust and my mother's sauce was like candy to me. She taught me so many things about cooking. She taught me to make the lentil soup that is loved by many of my guests and students. They often ask for the recipe. I know there was more than just ingredients in my mother's cooking. There was love. And her food was her way of showing us how much she loved us.

Castelcivita

The gift of the freedom to wander has also brought me to so many amazing places as I've traveled throughout Italy. As of now, I have probably driven at least 50,000 miles and visited countless numbers of small towns. I will always remember wandering into the town of Castelcivita in Campania, which was built into the stone and rock of the mountain. The town is extremely hilly, and it was difficult to determine which parts of the homes were man-made or which were part of the mountain. The streets were so small and narrow that sometimes they were simply steps that climbed to a farther, higher point of the town. The street numbers painted next to the doors were all single digits and the steps leading to the doors were carved right out of the rock, dating back to medieval times.

One day, as I walked along those narrow streets, I heard the sound of whistling echoing off the homes and rocks. I looked down the street to see where it was coming from and saw a petite, older woman happily making her way up the hill, whistling as she walked. Although she was missing several teeth, her whistle was deep and melodious like that of a songbird and she had one of the most beautiful smiles I'd ever seen. I imagine she must have been a fixture in the town, and there I was, just wandering, able to witness this gift of song to her fellow town dwellers. Her name is Angela Babbaro, and when I asked the mayor of the town, Antonio Forziati, if Angela does that often, he said to me *"Sempre!"* (always) and told me she has lived there all of her life.

What had brought me to Castelcivita was my desire to see the caves beneath the town and mountain, Grotte di Castelcivita. These caves were inhabited as far back as 42,000 years ago, making them the oldest known settlement in Europe. The caves crawl back into the mountain for almost two miles (about 3,000 meters), 1,200 meters of which can be traveled easily by tourists year-round. The next 1.1 miles (1,800 meters) are open from June to October, and have more challenging conditions.

During one of my many days of wandering, I was surprised and delighted by the tour I took of the caves. Even though the caves are much smaller than the caves in Carlsbad, New Mexico, which

The lady whistling in Castelcivita, Angela Babbaro.

I visited many years before, they are still very impressive, with beautiful clusters of stalagmites rising from the floor. There is one room that is referred to as "a kitchen" due to all the rock formations that resemble food, like a cluster that looked like a group of white mushrooms, and the lighting in the cave provides dramatic effects.

There was another young man and a couple on the cave tour with me that day. After the tour, I shared some of my leftover perishable food from the apartment I had checked out of that morning with the young man. He was a chef from Germany, en route to meet his girlfriend in Greece. He had bought a Mercedes hatchback and added an old secretary in the back which stored all his cooking utensils, supplies, spices, and staples.

It was fun sharing stories of the places we'd both visited while eating the cheese, meats, honey, nuts, and fruit in the parking lot. That never would have happened to my old banking self!

Dubai, Toothpaste, Toothpaste, Toothpaste...

One beautiful day we decided to take a drive to the Lunigiana, a mountainous area, in search of the place where the famous Carrara, Statuario, and Calacatta marbles are quarried. The Lunigiana region has had a turbulent history as far back as the Roman Republic. The fighting was finally settled with the rise of the Florentine state in the early 15th century. At that time, laborers quarried statuary or *statuario* marble there, just as the Romans had done many centuries before. The name serves as a reminder that some of the world's greatest statues, including Michelangelo's David, are made from this marble.

We had gone there because my friend Candida had planned to take some visiting friends from England on a day trip to Carrara. Since I had rented a minivan, I suggested I'd drive Candida and her guests. Frannie and I thought it would be interesting to see a part of Tuscany we hadn't seen yet. We picked up our friends and started the 1½-hour drive from our town to Carrara.

We approached Carrara near lunchtime and came upon a little town called Colonnata. We drove to the center of town with its tiny piazza that was completely paved in white marble. We decided to get some nourishment and settled in at the Ristorante Venanzio. The place was founded around 1970 by Venanzio Vannucci, a famous producer and exporter of a delicacy called *lardo di Colonnata*.

That day there was a Porsche club meeting, which gave us the opportunity to look at all the exotic cars parked in the square. I imagined how amazing it would have been to drive one of those babies up the mountain.

Our little group was delighted ordering and tasting the various offerings as we conversed with Candida and her friends. The wine and the bruschetta with tomatoes and lard was particularly delicious. Wanting to get a close look at the mountain where the marble is mined, Candida asked our friendly waiter if he knew anyone who could show us around. After a quick phone call, he told us to be waiting outside the restaurant at 4:00 p.m. for a guide.

As we waited for our guide to arrive, a dusty old pickup pulled up beside us, and a man stepped out to greet us. This was no ordinary guide. In fact, he wasn't a guide at all. His name was Luciano and he was the foreman of a crew working on the mountain. Sure, he wasn't an official legal tour guide, but what better guide can you have than a guy who has worked all of his life in the quarry?

When we reached the foot of the quarry, we parked our van and piled into his marble dust-covered, dated Nissan pickup to travel the rest of the way up the mountain. Frannie sat on my lap as we swerved off the main road and onto the work roads. We gasped at

Above: Mountains with Carrara marble near Colonnata, Italy.
Below: Marble mine.

~ 89 ~

the drop-offs to our right as we held on for dear life to minimize being tossed about in the back seat.

Finally, we stopped at the top. Luciano explained that the mountain is owned by 20 families who have been removing the precious white marble to sell it around the world for hundreds of years. Today, there's not much left of the high-quality Carrara, Statuario and Calacatta marble. Whatever good stuff remains is sold off to Dubai, which is the usual highest bidder. For every 5-ton highest-quality marble block cut from the mountain, there are four others of poor quality which are sold off to be used in the production of toothpaste.

We observed Luciano as he explained in his thick Lunigian dialect, "Dubai, toothpaste, toothpaste, toothpaste, toothpaste!"

He went on to say that the mine was almost depleted now, and the men have to work hard to find what little precious pieces of marble are left.

In ancient times men used just a hammer, chisel, and some small tools to hand-cut the stone. Luciano sat down to demonstrate to us how time-consuming the old methods were. Today, the men drill deep holes at the top of the stone and saw lengths of it using a diamond-laden saw band. They place soft metal bladders that can be expanded with water like wedges inside the cut marble. The hydraulic pressure forces apart the two sides and splits the huge chunk of marble like firewood.

This type of work has always been historically dangerous and today accidents happen often, including loss of life. By the end of the 19th century, Carrara had become a cradle of anarchism in Italy, in particular among the quarry workers. While learning about the area, I read a *New York Times* article from 1894, telling how workers in the marble quarries were among the most neglected laborers in Italy. Many of them were ex-convicts or fugitives from justice. The work at the quarries was so tough and arduous that almost any aspirant worker with sufficient muscle and endurance was employed, regardless of their background. Due to its brutal labor history, it's no wonder that Carrara is the birthplace of the International Federation of Anarchists (IFA), formed in 1968. After learning this, it made sense that the immigration officials asked my grandfather if he was an anarchist when he arrived at Ellis Island.

Both the mountain and the town had a strange feel to it. The town and surrounding area seemed to be closed off from the rest of Italy, as if the people there didn't want outsiders (anarchist and tourist alike) coming in to see what was going on. Maybe that's the result of 100-plus years of anarchists coming there to set a foothold. The mountain, in all its beauty, had a tired feel to it, as if to say "I've given you the best of me."

Today, it doesn't seem possible to make such a radical change to an environment as the one that has happened to this mountain. Different families, as Luciano put it, own different parts of the mountain. Some own the top, some own the sides, and some even own what's in the middle. It's not uncommon to see cave-like cuts in the mountain, where the workers cut the stone and harvest what is inside, while tons of marble lay above. I felt nervous just standing inside one of these caves, wondering how it is possible that the mountain doesn't just collapse around us.

Our guide was quite the entertaining character as he conducted this most informal but interesting tour. He had even created a little marble gift shop out of his truck bed, which he opened for us to browse through after our tour.

Luciano then offered to take us to his home to try his homemade wine and purchase some of the *lardo* he had cured. This area is known for its *lardo,* a type of cured pig fat that is served on warm toast so it melts the fat into the bread. It is salty and very delicious. We agreed, tasted his wine, and I purchased some of the *lardo.* He explained that the marble workers expended extra energy with all the heavy work they did during their daily duties, so they needed extra fat, especially during the winter months. *Lardo* was the perfect provider for this and it was tasty.

As we left Luciano's home, I noticed the inside of our minivan was covered with marble dust, brought in by our shoes as a departing gift. Now, when I see the famous David statue and other great marble works, I'll always think of our visit to the mountain just as Michelangelo had done, to personally pick out his raw stone for his works.

There are so many other stories I can recall over the past seven years that could fill this book completely. But I think these particular stories point out just how valuable it is to own your own time. As I mentioned earlier in this book, my son, Tony, was very helpful to me when I started my business. At that time, when I had made the decision to venture out full-time in my new business, I said to Tony, "Son, if this goes well, I will have hundreds of fond memories, some of which I might have forgotten, when the time comes that you will need to take care of me."

Well, I was right about the memories, but since I found a way to get paid for doing something I love to do, I don't think he will need to take care of me financially when I'm old. Fortunately, my clients know the value of my work and compensate me in both non-monetary and monetary ways. The memories we create together make me a very rich person indeed.

Chapter 7

MY NEW SICILIAN FAMILY

B y far, the greatest reward for transitioning from my old lifestyle and career was the development of a deep and loving relationship with my family members in Montelepre, Sicily. Although I was 50 years old before I ever met this side of my family, it seems like I've lived a lifetime with them in these last ten years. If not for this family, I wouldn't have had the authentic Italian travel experience. Over the years, my "new" family became my teachers of Italian and Sicilian cultures and provided an informal, but just as impactful, cooking school for me.

There were times I would ask, "Vita, teach me how to make your caponata!" or "Vitanna, show me how to make arancini!" I've had my very own cooking school in the hills of Sicily, making pizzas in Vita and Pino's backyard stone oven, and learning how to make macaroni with Vita's friend whom I call "Little Maria."

Luciana, the cousin I met the day after the big family dinner on my first trip to Italy, has become like a sister to me. She is the one I contact before my visits each year and she arranges the family get-togethers every time I visit. She also arranges other activities for me, like escorting me around Palermo and to the town where my mother was born. Her guidance and connection to other members of our family always provides me with countless stories of my travels to share with my friends and family members back in the States.

A Culinary Dream Come True

After many years of visiting and being served delicious Sicilian meals by my cousins, I finally declared that it was my turn to cook the Sunday dinner. I decided to prepare some of the courses we had served from the *How Italian Food Conquered the World* dinner at Ciao Bella Productions, our dinner theater company.

First, Luciana and her daughter, Alba, and I visited the famous Palermo outdoor market, Mercato di Ballarò, where we bought the eggplant and cheeses to create the *melanzane di involtini* (eggplant rollatini). Now, this market doesn't have the grandeur and style of the markets in larger cities like Florence or Rome, but it's still an experience. To watch the vendors and listen as they bark out, selling their goods and their exchanges with the hordes of visitors that shop there daily—it is theater! There is so much to see. Booth after booth of the most incredible array of foods, all fresh and locally sourced, and there every day. Tables spill over with fragrant, colorful, beautiful, and sometimes unusually shaped fruits and vegetables.

Lovely cuts of meat and a variety of sausages spread out over meat counters. Butchers, like characters from a Federico Fellini film, guard their goods, cleaver in one hand, cigarettes dangling from their mouths, ashes dropping who knows where. No American obsessions with cleanliness here, just people shopping for food as they have for hundreds of years.

The fishmonger's seafood simply can't be matched anywhere in the world, with the bounty of fish plucked from the Mediterranean each day. The clams are so fresh they're still moving around

Swordfish at the Palermo food market.

Seafood at the Palermo Ballaro food market

in their water-filled containers. That day, we saw an impressively giant *pesce spada* (swordfish) with its head turned upward and its long sword pointing to the sky on display across the counter. The butchers (or fish cutters) custom-cut the swordfish for their customers right there.

After the shopping was done, our prize-filled bags in hand and the mission accomplished, we were in need of a little refreshment. A visit to a nearby gelateria was in order.

Sicily has been blessed with the foods of its conquerors, and gelato is a perfect example. This frozen treat was first brought there by the Arab people when it was an Emirate of the Islamic Empire from 800 A.D. to 1090 A.D. An early form of a dessert was made with snow (not milk) brought down from the mountain and mixed with crushed fruit and honey. Hundreds of years later, the first gelato machine was invented in Sicily, which helped set this little island on a course to be the best dessert region in all of Italy.

For me, it was Amaretto with biscotti and for Alba vanilla and cocoa. We relaxed and cooled down with our wonderful servings of gelato and discussed our next task at hand.

We then drove up the mountain to the market to pick up the order we had called in for veal, prosciutto, and Fontina cheese for the *Saltimbocca alla Romana* (veal). I remembered the butcher, Giuseppe, from the year before. I watched with great marvel and envy as he skillfully butchered a chicken. While there, we grabbed some *semolina* (flour) and eggs for fresh pasta to complete the ingredients for the meal.

I must admit, I was a little nervous taking on the challenge of cooking for my family. When the number of guests climbed to around 25, I wondered how we would pull it all together. However, I had plenty of helpful cousins, and soon we were in a groove. Along with the veal and eggplant, I prepared two types of pasta and sauces. First, a simple basil marinara with spaghetti. Giuseppe, the son-in-law of our hosts Pino and Vita, offered to help roll the veal, ham, Fontina cheese and *salvia* (freshly-picked sage) from Pino's garden. Pino was enlisted to finish rolling and cutting the two types of pasta. Annalisa and Luciana assisted with the sauces and Vita was right by my side, grilling the veal on the outdoor kitchen stove.

Additionally, to give tribute to cooking in Sicily, we made a pistachio cream sauce over fettuccine. Italian cooks commonly use ground nuts in sauces, and pistachio is often preferred in Sicily. I have made this dish for at least 1,000 people and most say they've never heard of it, let alone eaten it.

Pino Barone making fresh pasta.

However, they love it and usually request the recipe. I think this common dish, eaten particularly on the eastern side of Sicily, is unknown in America because at the turn of the 20th century the pistachio must have been a rare commodity in the States. It makes sense that red sauce was dominant since tomatoes were readily available in places like New York City. Pistachios grown in the town of Bronte, Sicily are some of the finest in the world, and used to make pesto, seafood dishes, and especially desserts throughout the country. You'll find recipes in the back of this book for Pistachio Cream Sauce, Saltimbocca alla Romana, and Eggplant Rollatini.

Typically, in Sicily, fruit is served after the meal and before the dessert. Earlier that day, I had picked up a giant watermelon from a street vendor that I then cut into slices and served on a platter. For dessert, I had previously prepared a sheet of baklava to pay tribute to the Greeks who contributed a great deal to Italian cooking, along with fresh biscotti, prepared in a Tuscan style. This, combined with an amazing *torta gelato* (ice cream cake) that my cousin brought to the party, completed our feast.

My culinary dream came true when my family and our guests delivered a round of applause for the meal. What started many years ago as a desire to cook in Italy and to buy ingredients from the small town my grandfather was born in, culminated in a true cultural event. To gather, prepare, cook, and serve my family with all the love that radiates from food felt like a gift from God.

The Mediterranean Sea and a Look at the Past
You can't spend any length of time in Sicily without a day at the beach. One of my favorite places to visit is Cefalù, with its historic past and beautiful coastline.

One morning, my cousin Luciana and I ventured out early along the *autostrada* to head east into the rising sun. What a joy it is traveling on the highway that runs the northern perimeter of Sicily! There are times when I feel disappointed about the ineffectiveness of the Sicilian government's ability to provide adequate services for its citizens, like garbage removal, for example. But the freeways are a different story.

I am amazed by the structures that hold up the freeways in the skies across Italy. Constructed to withstand earthquakes and span long distances, Sicilian bridges are beautiful to look at as well as to drive on. The tunnels that cut through the rock and mountainsides seem to go on for miles. You have to wonder just how difficult it was to complete such a series of tunnels. As you travel through them and come out the other end, your eyes adjust to the bright Sicilian sun sparkling on the beautiful Mediterranean Sea. It is glorious.

Now, if you ever want to visit Cefalù, I highly recommend you avoid the month of August, the busiest month of the year. Car after car line the road leading into town, and you'll have a challenge just trying to find a parking space. Fortunately for us, we were invited to Luciana's cousin's villa by the sea for a Sicilian-style barbecue. Our delightful hosts, Valeria and Nunzio, escorted us to the beach, and then later into town.

Cefalù showcases many perfect examples of Sicily's past. The town and surrounding area still possess many of the architectural structures that were constructed in the 9th and 10th centuries by the Arabs, and 11th and 12th centuries by the Norman occupation. A laundry where people brought their garments to wash more than 1,000 years ago sits in the center of town. This interesting artifact is tucked down into a cave-like area and looks pretty much the same as when it was in use.

The Norman cathedral is just another example of the mosaic, biblical story-telling beauty that is typical of Norman Sicilian churches. Again, one has to wonder how such a magnificent work of art could be constructed back then in such a remote place in the world. When the churches were built, most of the people could not read and therefore these mosaics had to tell the stories from the Bible for them.

Shortly after our arrival at Luciana's cousin's, Nunzio put me on the back of his Vespa with our beach gear and we headed to a more secluded area for swimming. The sea was glistening in the sun, and floating in the heavily salted water was a spa-like experience.

On our way home we stopped at the market to pick up the fish we had reserved, knowing it was the freshest possible. Somehow Nunzio managed to get our *branzino* (sea bass) for the same price as the lower-priced salmon. It was some sort of Sicilian way of negotiating a better deal. I once witnessed this skill as a child on a visit to California with my grandfather when he purchased a guitar.

Back at the villa near the sea, Nunzio's wife, Valeria, was busy making a tomato-based zucchini soup, with potato and carrots, pairing it with a wonderful tossed salad. As soon as we arrived, Nunzio fired up the charcoal barbecue in the outdoor kitchen. He simply put the fish on the hot fire for about seven minutes on each side, then he combined olive oil, lemon, salt, pepper, and some Italian herbs to create a seasoning oil. It was amazing, dipping the fresh, tasty Sicilian bread into the soup, then eating his grilled sea bass. Fruit followed, of course, and then dessert.

Over lunch we discussed my desire to visit the town of Gualtieri Sicaminò, the birthplace of my mother. I wanted to find documentation of her birth. Nunzio delighted in helping me, and even offered to drive to the town, about an hour away.

The following morning, we arrived in Gualtieri Sicaminò. Small and situated against the Mediterranean, it looked quaint and pristine, like another train-set town. First, we visited the church to search for any baptismal records. The priest in charge asked for my contact information, and said he would try to email me anything he could find. We had much better luck at the City Hall where we met a genuinely nice lady sitting at a desk, surrounded by several

Birth record book for 1925 with
Carmela Mannino-Gaglio's birth record
in Gualtieri Sicaminò.

bookshelves containing birth records dating back more than 200 years. And there it was on the shelf—the book for 1925, the year my mother was born! As the clerk turned each page, I was excited to see if, indeed, my mother's birth was recorded. Sure enough, Carmela Mannino was listed as the 61st child born that year in the month of October. Not only did it include my mother's name, but it listed her parents' names and offered other information pertaining to my mother's family. It also noted that the child was not present during the recording. But everyone in town pretty much knew Rose Mannino had been expecting and had seen the baby.

What a special gift this was!

I thanked Nunzio profusely for assisting me. We took pictures, received a document certifying my mother's birth, and then drove down the street where my mother was born. Pretty much all the homes on this street and many others had been rebuilt since my mother's birth. The fact is, those former homes were so old, and the standards so poor, they could not have survived the years. But some old structures still remained on a hill along with new buildings, with views of the sea, making it a beautiful and diverse village.

As we drove higher up from the town, we noticed a very old, spooky-looking abandoned castle. Perched up high, it had an excellent view of the sea, which in the past provided good protection from any invaders coming from the water.

Luciana had been responsible for connecting me with our family in Sicily, and we quickly became very close. I felt so thankful for her and became close with her children, Alba and Vincenzo, as well. One year, I remember taking Vincenzo and another cousin, Roberto, all around the western end of Sicily for some sightseeing. The boys were in their early 20s and could speak a little English so they were immensely helpful to me as we traveled the island. We visited places like Marsala, known for its wine, which is wonderful both for cooking and as a tasty aperitif.

English trader John Woodhouse popularized Marsala wine after taking it to England in 1773. The fortified wine traveled well during long-distance journeys because the added alcohol kept it from spoiling. Marsala has sandy beaches and ferries that go to the nearby Aegadian Islands. This was the site of Giuseppe Garibaldi's landing on May 11, 1860, which was the beginning of the process of Italian unification. There are salt evaporation ponds there, still in use on the shoreline, continuing a practice of harvesting salt as it has been done for thousands of years.

We stopped to see the unfinished Elymian Greek Temple in Segesta, where a Greek theater also remains. The history of Sicily is so rich and deep, and Segesta is a great place to learn about the Greek period there.

Then we were off to Erice, which turned out to be one of my favorite places in Sicily, the history of which goes back to the

Luciana teaching me how to make tiramisú.

Phoenicians and is a beautiful example of a medieval Sicilian mountain town. The resort beaches of San Vito Lo Capo, Castellammare del Golfo, and Trapani were also among the stops we made.

I felt so thankful for Luciana, and to show her my thanks, I wanted to bring her to visit me in Sarasota as a Christmas gift for both of us. It was in Florida that Luciana taught me how to make *tiramisù* (see recipe in the back of this book).

The story of how I learned to make *tiramisù* starts with the first meeting I had with my cousin Luciana in Palermo, Sicily. After that first traditional Sunday afternoon dinner that my son and I had with our newfound family members (Luciana wasn't there), Giovanna (her sister) insisted that she visit with my son and me later that evening.

As you might recall, I had promised to make dinner for a British couple working as religious tour translators who were staying at our hostel. I had invited Luciana to join us for some gelato afterwards. Later that night when we were about to enjoy gelato with our British guests, Luciana arrived with a friend. Since our guests were translators, they happily translated our conversation with my newly found cousin and her friend. I learned a little about her life in Palermo and I asked her many questions about our family. At the end of our visit when we said our goodbyes, Luciana had invited me to stay with her the next time I visited.

I can't quite explain just what that meant to me at that point in time. There was a sense that I was amidst an extraordinary moment, though I didn't really understand why at the time. I felt the inherent love that existed inside us as family members who had been separated by my grandfather's decision to migrate to America.

The following year, a few days before my beach resort stay in Mondello, a delightful sea town just inside Palermo, I did take up Luciana's invitation to stay with her and her daughter, Alba. We visited with other family members, and I met some of her children's friends. Luciana prepared a baked *anelletti* pasta dish for us, which is very popular in Palermo and generally reserved for holidays.

The little round *anelletti* pasta is parboiled, combined with the other ingredients, and then baked in the *forno* (oven) with a *ragù* (meat) sauce. This hearty pasta dish also contains beef, peas, tomato sauce and grated Parmesan, Romano, and mozzarella cheeses. The simple flavors of basil, oregano, garlic, salt, and pepper give it that Sicilian flair, and the onions and chopped zucchini add additional flavor and body. This is topped off with breadcrumbs (or bread dough) and high-quality olive oil before it's baked. It was the first time I had had this dish, and it was even more special because it was prepared by my cousin, Luciana.

One year, before I returned home from Sicily, I saw a Disney poster in Alba's bedroom, and I asked her if she had liked to watch Disney movies when she was a child. She said she loved them and had visited Disneyland in Paris.

After several years of visiting Luciana and her children, I wanted to host them in my Sarasota home. I wanted to return the hospitality she had given me, and her parents had given my parents so many years earlier. I surmised that, as a single mother, it would be difficult for Luciana to travel with her children. As a Christmas present (mostly to myself), I proposed I would spring for their travel arrangements, looking forward to a Christmas with family. Anticipating Luciana might resist, I instructed Vincenzo to tell his mother that this had been decided and to insist she go along with my plan.

For years, when I lived in Michigan with my family, we hosted holiday dinners in my home. After many years of living alone in Sarasota, I longed for the opportunity to have family with me during the holidays. What better way to accomplish this than sharing my world with my Sicilian cousins?

I planned all kinds of activities for their stay. They enjoyed trips to the Ringling and the Dali museums, *The Nutcracker* ballet, the children's circus, a play at the Florida Studio Theater and, of course, boating and the beach. I even arranged a four-night stay at Disney World to visit all the parks (I skipped all but one of those days). We had an amazing visit and my "gift" to myself was truly appreciated by my cousins. Alba later wrote to tell me how special it was to again spend every day eating meals together and spending time with her brother and mother.

We cooked a great deal in my apartment. On Christmas Eve Day, Luciana taught me how to prepare *tiramisù* with ingredients we gathered from the Sarasota Italian market. I watched her carefully prepare the coffee, the mascarpone cheese and the whipped cream. (Whipped cream is not in the traditional Venetian recipe; however, cream is used a lot in Sicilian cooking. It's possible the French control of the island in its past influenced the use of cream in recipes. The Spanish royalty also brought in French chefs during the time of the Spanish control of Sicily.)

Luciana then topped the layers with cocoa and dark chocolate and we carefully placed it in the refrigerator for Christmas dinner the next day.

We then took off for Christmas Eve dinner and a midnight church service at one of Sarasota's non-denominational congregations, where an awesome rock band performed. Coming from Italy, a country where 98 percent of the people are Roman Catholic, my cousins were blown away with excitement during the services. Never had Luciana, Alba, nor Vincenzo been to such a worship service before. With the lights turned off, holding lit candles and singing songs with the faithful worshipers, we knew we were having a most memorable experience.

The next day at Christmas dinner, I was excited to try our dessert. When we finally ate it, I realized it was the best I had ever eaten. And I'm not alone. So many times, people tell me at my events and dinners where I serve *tiramisù* that "It's the best I've ever had" or "I normally don't like *tiramisù*, but yours isn't too sweet." I tell them it's not my recipe; it's Luciana's.

The reason is that her *tiramisù* lacks the overuse of sugar added to the whipped cream and mascarpone cheese. The ladyfinger cookies are already coated on one side with sugar, so to add more just makes the dessert too sweet and rich. Instead, you enjoy the taste of coffee, vanilla, the mascarpone and the light and delightful whipped cream. Although this recipe differs from what would be served in Venice, I always make it this way because it's so good!

Just a few years after that visit, a great sadness overtook my Sicilian family when we lost Luciana to illness. In such a short time, Luciana and I created so many wonderful memories. So, now, when people enjoy the *tiramisù* I serve, it warms my heart to know that she still lives inside me, forever. What I thought was a gift to myself on just one Christmas turned into a lifelong gift and now I get to remember Luciana every time I serve *tiramisù*.

I always say, "Food is love." The lesson of making *tiramisù* with Luciana was a gift of love I received and will always cherish.

That was a tough year, just a few months before losing Luciana, I had lost my father. I was blessed to have my father for so many years, but I felt just as blessed to have found Luciana, and our love for each other had grown every year. In only five years we packed in many experiences, and if it wasn't for her, I don't think I could have created the relationships I now have with my other family members back in Sicily.

Spending time at my cousin Vita's country home in the mountains has been some of the most cherished times I've ever had in Italy as well. Once when I had just gotten there for a visit, I noticed Vita's neighbor preparing tomatoes for canning in her yard under the Sicilian sun. She was doing it just as I had imagined it from that first day in Montelepre when my new friend, Joanna, told me how they are prepared.

It has been so much fun visiting there in the summer and fall each year. Luciana's sister, Vitanna, is such an amazing cook also; it's always a feast when I go there for a meal. She taught me how to make the traditional *arancino,* a typical Sicilian street-food item. I love to stop at the butcher shop to pick up meat and have Vitanna's son, Roberto, barbecue it on the patio while Vitanna prepares the other courses. One year, I had a few guests with me before our Sicilian tour started, and I brought them over to Vitanna's house where we cooked for my cousins. As American tourists they had an incredible experience and I feel so blessed I get to do this every year for people in my new life.

My relationships with my family continued to grow even though I lost my precious cousin, Luciana, and that connection has even formed with the newer generation, which are my father's third cousins. Some of them, whom I call *ragazzi* and *ragazze* (boys and girls), have become so special to me, and it has allowed me some important emotional growth and experience. Those kids have touched my life in lasting and permanent ways.

A Parent's Love

I am a member of a generation where it was very common for families to consist of five, eight or even ten or more children. As a child, I remember many families on the block who were larger than my own, and I was the youngest of five. Before I was a parent myself, I wondered how it was possible for a parent to have enough love for a family so large.

I often think of my grandfather's family in turn-of-the-century Montelepre, and the hardship they faced just to provide food for their family. In the cultural and culinary classes I teach in Sarasota about Italy and Sicily, I always include discussion of the mass migration of Sicilians to other countries in search of a better life. During the period from 1890 to 1910, it is estimated that about five million Sicilians left their country of about 25 million. A few times I've been asked by my students, "Why did so many people leave?"

The answer to this question became very clear as I learned what my great-grandmother had to deal with back then. You see, I always knew my grandfather had three brothers and a sister; he and two of his brothers were part of that great migration to the United States of

America. However, there was much more to the story of my grandfather's family that I only discovered while searching for his birth certificate.

My uncle Gus, in California, had provided me with an incorrect birth year. Therefore, when I had gone to the town clerk with my friend Carlo, the clerk couldn't find the record of his birth, stating that there wasn't a record associated with his name on that day. I remembered a padre in town, who gave me a family tree of my grandfather's family dating all the way back to the 1680s. I had suggested to Carlo that maybe he could help us.

It turned out that Padre Gaspare Randazzo is well known in the town as an expert of genealogy for Montelepre, and has created a large database of the families there. Padre Randazzo not only provided me with the correct year of my grandfather's birth, but also informed me that my great-grandmother, Antonia Mónaco Gaglio, actually gave birth to ten children, not just the five I was aware of. One by one, Padre Randazzo showed me the computer screens from his database with the information about the children of my great-grandmother. For example, there was Salvatore Gaglio, who was born on April 19, 1896, but didn't survive his second birthday. His death date was December 2, 1897. Angela Gaglio, and her fraternal twin, Salvatore (the second given that name), were Christmas babies born on December 24, 1898. Salvatore only survived one night and Angela passed away a few days later on December 28th. I was confused with Salvatore's information, because I remember great-uncle Sal (born in 1903), but realized that people back then just reused the name again to honor a relative, as was the case of my great-uncle Sal.

The chart below details the births and deaths of the children of Antonia Mónaco, my great-grandmother:

Name	Date of Birth	Date of Death
Vita Gaglio	7/09/1886	6/16/1888
Giuseppe Gaglio	4/07/1888	1/06/1889
Vita Gaglio (2nd Vita)	10/26/1889	Lived to Adulthood
Giuseppe Gaglio (2nd Giuseppe)	1/09/1892	Lived to Adulthood
Francesco Gaglio	3/28/1894	Lived to Adulthood
Salvatore Gaglio	4/19/1896	12/2/1897
Salvatore Gaglio (2nd Salvatore)	12/24/1898	12/25/1898
Angela Gaglio	12/24/1898	12/28/1898
Gioacchino Gaglio	10/15/1900	Lived to Adulthood
Salvatore Gaglio (3rd Salvatore)	11/02/1903	Lived to Adulthood

This information reflects the dramatic poverty in Sicily at the time, with its high mortality rates among newborns and young children. It's no wonder my grandfather boarded a ship from Palermo at age 18 and headed for New York City. My great-uncles Jack and Sal also left for the United States, with the possibility of never returning to see their mother and father again.

Can you imagine a mother's sorrow as she watched three of her sons who survived such harsh conditions sail off to a faraway land? My grandfather did return, though, after two world wars, and I have a photograph of him in 1949 next to his mother exhibiting a smile filled with love for her long-missed son. I have no doubt that my great-grandmother would have had plenty of love for each and every one of her children if all ten had survived.

I have two children, whom I love with all my heart, but I also know I have enough love to share with many more. I've had the amazing experience of forming relationships with some of my younger cousins in Sicily, which has taught me that I am capable of giving an unlimited amount of love. It's possible that the reason I've been on this path is not only to share such love within me, but to receive it as well. Three young cousins in particular have become so special to me and I hope I've made an impact on their lives as well.

Emanuela

I met Emanuela on my first visit to Sicily when she was 18 years old, just before she had lost her dad to cancer and finding herself without him to help her into adult life. Over the years, we have become very close as she has helped me communicate with my other cousins through her translations, particularly after Luciana passed away. During this time, she was contemplating what to do about her future. I invited her to spend a week on tour with us in Tuscany interacting with our tour guides to see if the travel industry would be of interest to her. I also wanted her to be able to enjoy a part of Italy she had never seen before.

On another visit she opened up her closet to my daughter, who is the same age, when some of Kaitlyn's luggage failed to arrive at the Palermo airport.

A few years later, Emanuela decided to enter the military, like her father had done when he was a young man. That skinny, shy, 18-year-old I had met on the mountain in Sicily has turned into a confident and physically strong young woman, who speaks English with great ease. After fulfilling her duty in the Italian military and completing her academy work, I am proud to say she is now a member of the Carabinieri. This is Italy's trusted and prestigious law enforcement institution. It's hard to express the amount of joy I got when she texted me a photo of her and her family at her mother's birthday party. They were about to celebrate with a bottle of wine I had given her mother on a recent visit. It also warmed my heart waking up on my birthday to my first birthday greeting sent by Emanuela during the night.

The photos of us during that first dinner together on the mountain show my son sitting next to Emanuela's father. I truly believe it was a sign that someday I would be there supporting her in ways fathers do because he wouldn't be with her for much longer. I can't help but feel there is a role I have in her life—to help fill the loss of her father.

Riccardo

Another cousin, Riccardo, lives in London now, having graduated with a master's degree in finance. We made a connection given our educational backgrounds, and through the years I have become very close to his mother, Vitanna, as well as his brothers, Roberto and Emanuele. Riccardo lost his father when he was a boy living in Campania and his mother moved the family back to Montelepre.

Riccardo and I have had great culinary adventures over the years. It's always fun to meet him in London or other places like Barcelona where we do food tours and indulge in elegant dinners. One time, we did our best to eat as much seafood in Barcelona as we could. Riccardo's friend recommended a place for lunch, O'Retorno, where locals go to enjoy a favored dish of octopus with potatoes. The paprika seasoning was the best I've ever tasted and the octopus was cooked to perfection. Watching the locals during their lunch-time was interesting as well.

One of my favorite experiences with Riccardo was the time in London when he told me he wanted to try to golf at a place near his home. I was confused, and asked, "How could there be a golf course in the middle of London?"

He couldn't quite explain it, but when we arrived at the place, I realized it was only a driving range. Riccardo had never placed a golf club in his hands before, let alone tried to hit a golf ball with one, so there I was, giving him a quick lesson on how to swing a golf club. Now, I'm the last person who should be giving a golf lesson, considering I've never come close to scoring under 100, but I was able to give him enough instruction for him to actually make contact and hit the ball pretty far. His mother really enjoyed the video I sent her of Riccardo's first attempt at a driving range.

Today, Riccardo has a good job in London in his chosen profession and I'm so proud of all of his accomplishments. It makes me happy to visit him and I look forward to treating him to wonderful foods and new experiences in the future.

Alba

Finally, there is my dear Alba, the daughter of my late cousin Luciana. When I brought Alba, her brother, and mother to Sarasota, we became very close and have continued to solidify our relationship over the past several years. It was a somber experience when I visited Alba in Montelepre after her mother passed away. It was the year before Alba was to graduate from college. There we were, sitting in her mother's kitchen, when I asked, "How are you, Alba? Do you have anyone to talk to about your mother's death?"

"I have my father," she said, "who lost his mother when he was young and the same with my boyfriend, who lost his father recently. However, I don't know how to make my mother's *tiramisù*."

At that moment, my heart spilled open and I suggested we go to the market and collect the ingredients and prepare the dessert for the family dinner the following night in the country. Later that day as we worked together making the dessert, Alba looked at me and said, "I feel my mother in the room when I'm with you." Holding back tears of grief, I smiled at Alba and thanked her for having me in her life; I felt such love from her, as if she were my own daughter.

There it was, the love in this family came full circle, with my grandfather leaving in 1912 and my returning just over 100 years later to teach my cousin, Alba, her mother's *tiramisù* recipe. So, to answer my initial question, "Can a parent have enough love for all their children, no matter how many?" The answer is definitely yes! It is clear to me through the experiences I've had with my young cousins in Sicily: a parent has no limits on the love he or she can share with a child. Like with my own children, my life has been deeply enriched through the relationships I share with Emanuela, Riccardo, and Alba. A parent has unlimited love, it seems to me, because we have been designed by God to be that way.

Introducing My Siblings to Our Sicilian Family

In recent years, I've had the enjoyment of bringing three of my siblings to Sicily to meet our family there. One year my two sisters, Fran and Roseann, stayed with me in a villa in a vacation town called Scopello. This small, picturesque village arose in the late 18th century around a *baglio* (traditional Sicilian farmhouse with a courtyard), on the site of a pre-existing rural Arab home. It now consists of a few shops, bars, and the famous artisan bakery, Di Stabile e Anselmo.

The area is visited mostly by vacationing Sicilians and other Europeans for its fresh country air, beautiful Mediterranean vistas, crystal-clear water, and many beaches.

We had arranged to have our extended family come to the villa for dinner so they could meet everyone. It was so much fun sharing great food, and we managed to speak to each other despite our limited knowledge of the other's languages. At one point my sister, Fran, said a phrase my father would say to my mother, "*e chi sacciu*" in Sicilian. The whole house broke out in laughter. This is an expression Sicilians use when someone is questioning something difficult or impossible to know. In that moment, I remembered the expression on my father's face as he said this to my mother's pestering questions. This was more evidence that even though 100 years separated us, we are the same. We are Sicilians.

In 2019, my brother, Joe, and I embarked on a road trip in Italy and then journeyed to meet with our cousins in Sicily. I had first picked up my brother in Rome and drove him straight to Sorrento for the night. It was Joe's first trip visiting Italy and I had a packed itinerary for him. First on the list was having dinner in Sorrento where, although it is a big tourist town, you can still find great places to eat without a long wait. I highly recommend, when visiting Sorrento, walking down to Marina Grande and finding a lovely restaurant overlooking the marina for a magical dining experience.

Next, we drove down the coast for a stop in Amalfi for a coffee. Joe was amazed at the crowds of tourists in October. The beautiful coastline gave many opportunities for Joe to take stunning photos, and although it may appear scary to drive, it isn't really that difficult.

The main tourist prize for me, and it turned out to be Joe's as well, was our next stop in the region of Basilicata, where the UNESCO World Heritage Site City of Matera is located. That year, Matera was also declared a European Capital of Culture. We hired a guide to take us through the internationally-famed Sassi di Matera, an area in the center of the city consisting of the caves people had lived in up to their evacuation in 1952. It is possible that this part of Italy was one of the first to be inhabited by humans, who dug out cave dwellings in the 10th millennium BC.

The caves remained empty until the late 1980s when the city administration created a more tourism-orientated zone by allowing shops, pubs, restaurants, hotels, and residences to be redeveloped inside the caves. Since then, the Sassi has become a quaint tourist attraction and a fascinating place to visit.

On our way to Sicily, we stopped at the remains of the Tavole Palatine, a late 6th-century Doric Greek temple dedicated to Hera. It is located in the archaeological area of Metapontum, in the "arch" of the Italian boot. Later that day we caught a car ferry to bring us over to Sicily where we stopped in Cefalù and then onward to meet up with our cousin, Vita, and her husband, Pino, at their home in Palermo.

As we drove into the Palermo city limits, my brother was amazed at my Sicilian driving skills and said there was no way he could manage the craziness. I've found that over the years, I've become a very good driver in Italy. However, it's made me a terrible driver in the U.S. Evidence of this are the two accidents I had within 30 days in March of 2017. Needless to say, my insurance was canceled at my renewal and the replacement cost twice as much.

When we reached Vita's home, she had prepared a large dinner for us including caponata, fresh pasta with red sauce, and lots of fresh ricotta cheese, and a meatloaf stuffed with eggs, cheese, and breadcrumbs, topped with a gravy. You roll the ingredients in the meat and dip it in egg wash and then breadcrumbs. This is then fried in a pan and a sauce is made with onion, peas, and carrots. There was salad and, of course, many desserts.

After dinner, while we were enjoying our dessert, Vita showed us her wedding photo album from over 40 years ago. As we began to look through the photos, Joe came across a side profile photo of Vita in her wedding veil. It was a confirmation that we were related, since my brother's daughter looks almost identical to Vita at that age. Joe retrieved a photo of his daughter from his iPhone, which was taken from the same side, just like the photo of Vita, and it was stunningly similar to Vita's wedding photo.

Bringing my brother, Joe, sisters Roseann and Fran, and my brother-in-law, Larry, to Sicily was like completing the reconstruction of the two families. Although the distance remains, we will now always be connected as family.

Chapter 8

NEW FRIENDS

Ever since I left the corporate world and began sharing my Italian travel experiences with guests, I realized one of the greatest gifts has been meeting people and making friends along the way. Sure, seeing beautiful places, amazing works of art, tasting delicious foods and wines have been pleasing experiences for me as well. However, the opportunity to spend time with my family in Sicily and making new friends in Italy, has been the most rewarding. Along this journey, I have made many new friends, who have greatly enriched my experiences in Italy.

Silvia, Gabriele and Maria Rosa Solé

Since the very beginning, my decision to travel to Italy that first time has resulted in making new friends. The first friend I made wasn't someone I met in Italy, but rather someone I met right after I returned home from my first trip.

I walked into my Rotary Club lunch meeting and there was an unfamiliar couple sitting alone at a table, so I decided to sit with them and introduce myself. Coincidentally, the couple, Silvia and Gabriele, were vacationing from Magenta, Italy, which is located about 30 miles east of Milan. I explained that I had just returned from Italy for the first time and mentioned I had met some of my family still living there in Sicily.

Silvia was visiting our club and was a Rotary Club member in Magenta. They were there to enjoy the beaches on Longboat Key, Florida. Soon, my Rotarian friend, Nick, walked in, who also is Italian-American and was planning his first trip to Italy later that fall. So, I asked him to sit down with us so he could get to know Silvia and Gabriele. During the lunch, both Nick and I asked the couple many questions about Italy, and we learned that Silvia was a high school teacher and Gabriele was an emergency response professional. Since this was their first visit to our community, Silvia asked me, "Where is a good place to eat?"

To which I replied, "My place!" Silvia thought I meant I owned a restaurant, so I laughed and told her, "No, I want you to come to my house for dinner." A few days later, I cooked for them as well as Nick and that was the beginning of our long and wonderful friendship.

Over several visits to her home in Magenta, Silvia has taken me to many places around her city. Through her I discovered the amazing city of Milan. It is not the first city that comes to mind when people plan to visit Italy, but there is so much to see and do there. The city is a mixture of old and new structures, from its modern design and fashion center to the classic treasures like the Duomo di Milano, Galleria Vittorio Emanuele II, and Il Cenacolo (The Last Supper).

The Duomo di Milano is one of my favorite cathedrals to visit because of its extraordinary exterior. I will always remember climbing to the rooftop with Silvia and taking in the eye-level views of the spectacular pinnacles, spires, and some of the sculptures that would otherwise be unobservable. From there, you get a view of the city, the Galleria Vittorio Emanuele II (Italy's oldest active shopping gallery), and the Teatro Alla Scala, which is across the piazza from the Galleria. The Galleria is a jewel, with the glass dome sheltering the facades, statues, mosaics, and 19th-century iron-and-glass architecture.

On another visit, Silvia took me to Lake Como, where we took a ferry boat from the City of Como to Bellagio for lunch. It happened to be a spectacularly sunny morning and the view of all the little towns and villages along the shore was breathtaking. Bellagio is perched upon the cape that divides Lake Como in two and has the Italian Alps as a backdrop. The combination of Bellagio's location on the shore of the lake with the mountains in the background, and its charming old hotels and homes make it the quintessential Italian postcard setting.

The most special times I've had with Silvia and Gabriele are the times we've gathered together for the home-cooked meals Silvia's mom, Maria, prepared for us. She always insists on having me at her dinner table and refuses to let me cook (which I happily oblige). I just sit back and watch her prepare risotto like only a Lombardian can.

Antonella, Luigi and Carla

The friendship I share with Antonella, our singer/performer who entertains our guests each week in Tuscany, has blossomed. Our guests in Italy sometimes dine at her boyfriend Luigi's restaurant, where I have had the opportunity to join the chef in the kitchen. Antonella's mother, Carla, taught me the art of making *orecchiette* pasta (translates as "small ears"). In reciprocal appreciation, I have hosted Antonella in Sarasota where she has performed for several guests, solidifying our ongoing friendship.

Loredana

These past five years, I've had the honor to get to know the owner of the beautiful villa that I rent in Tuscany for our group tours. Loredana is a hardworking, talented, and hospitable host. We delight in her delicious dinners served under the Tuscan sky. A forever student of learning Italian culture, I'm impressed with her ease in preparing risotto, a favored dish. Then there is her never-ending work on making the villa an amazing place to relax and take in all that Tuscany has to offer. Each year I return to another beautiful improvement to the 500-year-old villa. She is always there for our guests, making sure everything is perfect.

Candida's Tuscan Garden

From the moment I met Candida, during my first tour in Tuscany, I felt a strong connection. I had needed a place to stay near the villa since I had a full house of guests. Loredana suggested the little bed and breakfast just at the top of the road that is owned and managed by her friend Candida. I booked a room in her cozy B&B and felt very comfortable staying in her home. I barely saw my new landlord that week since I was leaving early and coming back late each day. But when we did have the chance to share a coffee, I could tell there was something incredibly special about this woman.

Her grandfather was a Jewish German man who had settled in Florence and married a Tuscan woman near the turn of the century. In 1905, he started a hat manufacturing company producing hats for field workers. Through the years the company grew and began making a more diverse collection of hats. Candida's father continued with the business during the Second World War but had to move the ownership of the company into his partner's name because of his Jewish heritage.

After Candida had finished her schooling, which included a year of study in the United States, it was her turn to work with her father. They had a wonderful relationship, and he taught her many things about business and life.

She was a businesswoman, working in a man's world, creating hats. Yet, the business grew over the years. It went from making simple hats for field workers to making them for famous designers and movie stars. It took a special woman to succeed in that situation, but her creativity and tenacity made it possible.

Sadly, after 100 years in business, the pressures of the global economy and the world financial crisis brought an end to their hat company. Candida later settled in her home in San Casciano, where she now displays several of the hat molds the company had used in her living room. She has a wonderful vegetable and flower garden and some olive trees. She also has a collection of beautiful finches and songbirds in a walk-in aviary in the garden, and even some chickens that produce fresh eggs for her bed-and-breakfast guests.

She is a painter, jeweler, garden furniture dealer, amazing chef, and proprietor of a bed-and-breakfast, and never seems to rest. She has more talent than most people and shares it freely in so many ways. The paintings she creates decorate her lovely country home and several of our guests have purchased her original jewelry.

After meeting Candida, I thought it would be very special for our guests to share an evening at her dinner table. She delighted our guests with her cuisine, so she is now a regular part of the tour experience. She likes to share stories of her life and to show photographs of her family and beautiful new grandson. I really enjoy the photos from when she came to America as a teenager. One photo depicts President Kennedy addressing her group of students when they visited Washington, D.C.

Our friendship has been so endearing to me, and I always invite her to one of the villa parties we host each year. I love to cook for her and to see her enjoy the entertainment we provide our guests.

One year she invited me to have lunch with her friends on a Saturday afternoon. One of her friends was the former dean of philosophy for an American college. Another was Ferdinando, a brilliant and extremely cultured man whose family has been employed in the making of bronze and stone sculptures for four generations. In the 1940s, his grandfather made molds of some of Italy's greatest art, including Michelangelo's David and a collection of Etruscan works. This company is world-renowned. They even created the bronze broncos that adorn Mile-High Stadium where the Denver Broncos play.

Workers at the Ferdinando Marinelli Artistic Foundry, Florence, September 2017.

Today these molds are priceless because the curators of such works will never allow them to be created again. Fernando's clients come from all over the world. Many come from China seeking copies of Western art, which were systematically removed during the Communist revolution.

We were able to tour the foundry where artists work on the finishing touches of the statues poured weeks before. Just a few feet away the workers poured the molten bronze material into the molds buried in the compacted earth and water beneath the floor. Molten bronze is nine times heavier than water, so the earth needs to be very sturdy around the molds to prevent the bronze from breaking as it cools.

I'm sure Ferdinando had been bending his rules that day because he knew our group was fascinated by the precision and dedication that each artist puts into their work. We relished the opportunity to watch them work. Normal travel agencies would not be allowed to bring their clients so close to the actual process. So, to experience this was a privilege.

It's hard to conceive I could have ever replicated these friendships and experiences if I had never left the corporate world and started my little tour company. I am most grateful for the relationships I've formed and truly treasure my lasting friendships with these fascinating people.

The Matteuzzi Family and Their Grape Harvest

For six years now I've had the pleasure of cooking and serving our guests in Tuscany and drinking the wine of the Chianti region. The end of the 2019 tour season was especially exciting because I was invited to help pick the grapes at one of my favorite vineyards: The Matteuzzi Family Vineyard of Montoro e Selvole, located in Greve, in the Chianti region. This place has been one of the favorite experiences for many guests. They truly enjoy touring the property and walking through the grapevines and olive trees. The amazing food the family provides from their garden and their wonderful Chianti makes guests feel fully immersed in the Tuscan cultural experience.

Through the years, I've become very close to the Matteuzzi family and feel at home when we visit. It's fun to bring gifts from our villa "home." We treat the family with *caponata* (an eggplant dish) and

Robert harvesting grapes with the Matteuzzi family, Greve in Chianti, September 19, 2019.

fresh pasta made by our guests in cooking class, and bring a bottle of Chianti Tagefune wine, which is produced at the vineyard that surrounds the villa. Our guests are so appreciative and honored to be invited into their charming home and feel a sense of family throughout the experience.

This year on the last visit, they invited me to help pick the grapes on the following Sunday. I jumped at the chance. After all those years of walking through the vineyards of Montepaldi and visiting many farms, I had never had that experience. I wasn't going to pass up the opportunity.

It was Sunday morning, the day after a long month of tours. I was exhausted, to say the least, yet very energized to start the day. After breakfast, I journeyed to Greve to the farm just up the hill from the town. As I drove through the hills of the countryside, I took in the splendor of the landscape. There was just a hint of the change of season in the hills, with withering sunflower fields and some subtle changes in the color of the leaves. The trees don't provide the amazing array of fall colors like in the northeast of North America, but this landscape has its own beauty. As far as other motorists, I was all alone. However, there was no shortage of cyclists, no doubt preparing for the big race the following weekend in Gaiole in Chianti. It's very common to share the road with cyclists on Sundays, and with winter approaching, I'm sure many were hoping to get in their last rides before winter.

When I arrived, I was greeted by Manuela's husband, Sergio, and in my simple Italian I asked, "Dove sono Giovanni e Maurizio?" ("Where are Giovanni and Maurizio?")

Sergio pointed in the direction of the tractor and handed me a set of clippers that were sitting on a bench. The two were not far from the house, father and son picking grapes as they had done for decades. This time I had the honor of working beside them.

They were in the field with the Canaiolo grapes, which are blended with the Sangiovese to make the Chianti. I jumped right in, grabbing a basket and observing how they were clipping the stems of the grapes. The grandson, Enzo, joined us shortly after.

In my row, Maurizio managed the tractor, which supported a big stainless-steel bucket on the back. When our baskets were filled, we dumped the grapes into the bucket. The 86-year-old grandfather, Giovanni, was in the next row. When we had cleared ten or so vines, Maurizio would move the tractor forward, so we could continue harvesting more grapes.

Since the tractor was in my row, I could observe Giovanni's basket full of grapes before they were dumped into the bucket. Although I felt I was holding my own, he always seemed to have a much fuller basket than mine each time I dumped it. He reminded me of my high school best friend's father, Mr. Casasanta, who has a Christmas tree farm in Kalkaska, Michigan. I remember as a teenager being amazed by how hard he worked on his farm, just like Giovanni. Mr. Casasanta also taught me how to make fresh pasta in the basement of his home, something I will never forget.

It's as if hard work in the field is in their DNA. In Giovanni's case, he was born on this farm and began to work and learn to make wine at an early age. With little more than five years of formal education, this man managed to provide for his family through the farm. He also provided the possibility for his son to keep farming and created the foundation for his grandchildren to be able to obtain college degrees.

One grandson, Matteo, went to the University of Florence for winemaking. As part of his education, he worked at the vineyard at Montepaldi that surrounds the villa we use for our Tuscany tour. The school uses this location to teach future winemakers. Currently, Matteo is a junior winemaker at Castello Di Verrazzano, where we visit each year on our Tuscany Dream Tour.

As we continued to pick grapes, I really gained an understanding of them. The majority of the vines were full of large clusters that I estimated to weigh over a pound, while others had just a few or very little at all. A small portion of the vines had grape clusters that were dried out like raisins, which we discarded. Some were so ripe the juices would explode in my hands, coating my fingers in purple. My hands would display the evidence of my work in the field for several days after.

The work continued until the tractor bucket was full. Then, we walked behind the tractor as Maurizio drove it to the barn, which housed the crusher/de-stemmer. The bucket contents were slowly dumped into that loud machine that spits out the stems before crushing them and pumping the grape juice through a hose into the large, glass-lined fiberglass tank. There, it will ferment before being transferred to the barrel or holding tank.

We completed this process twice. Afterwards, we had lunch in the Matteuzzi family home with several other members of the family. At the table, I sat next to Matteo, who had returned from a bicycling trip in the area. He and his coworkers from Verrazzano were on a team scheduled to race the following weekend.

At lunch, I took delight in the home-cooked, roasted chicken raised in their own coop. The meal also included roasted potatoes and fagiolini (string beans, aka green beans) that were grown in their garden. Over lunch I asked Matteo questions about winemaking and picking the grapes:

"Why do some of the vines produce better fruit than others?"

"It could be the type of soil underneath the vine; maybe there are rocks that make it difficult to grow and seek water," he said. "In cases where there are dried-out, raisin-like fruit, it could be a fly that laid eggs on the fruit infecting it with a fungus. Grapes are like children in a group. When one gets sick, the ones around them get sick as well."

"Why do some of the same varieties of grapes produce larger fruit?" I asked.

"Some of the vines are old. When they are young, they produce large quantities of berries, but as they age, they produce fewer and fewer, however, with better quality," he explained. "Sometimes they make so few grapes, they need to be pruned back substantially so in a few years the new growth will again begin to produce quality fruit. When you prune, you have to prune for the present and for the future, making sure you don't cut the vine shoots that will produce the berries for next year and the following year after."

It was a fascinating and informative conversation and a delicious lunch as well. The lunch concluded with a sweet yellow cake with dried fruit. As we enjoyed our *dolce*, Matteo's brother, Enzo, suggested I return in the evening for his grandmother, Nonna Bruna's 86th birthday party. How could I resist? "Absolutely!" I said and told them I would return with a dessert in hand.

Before lunch ended, I asked if they had enjoyed the *caponata* our guests made for them. They said it was so good the younger family members consumed it before the grandparents could try some. I just happened to have a few jars in my car that I had packed for my next journey, so I ran to retrieve a jar just for Nonna as a birthday gift. She smiled with great joy.

After lunch, I drove to the Esselunga, the only store I could think of that would be open on a Sunday afternoon, to buy items I would need to make the dessert. I had decided I would make *baklava*, a Greek dessert, which is easy and doesn't take much time. My childhood friend, Dimitrios, taught me how to make it many years ago in Sarasota, where we had both ended up living as adults. I had some filo dough, pistachios, butter, and sugar back at the Bed and Breakfast, but I needed walnuts, vanilla, and honey (see Baklava recipe in the back of this book).

My dear bed-and-breakfast host, Candida, rounded up some wrapping paper, twine for a bow and a fresh flower to place in the middle of the dessert to make a perfect birthday gift. I was excited to see Bruna's face when she saw the beautiful packaging and tasted the scrumptious pastry. It turned out that only the grandson, Matteo, and his wife had ever had the dessert, when they visited Turkey.

To say I enjoyed the special birthday celebration would be such an understatement. We feasted on pizzas made in the stone oven outside by a son-in-law who is the chef for a local hotel. The *antipasti* meats were cut right on the kitchen counter with the family's own deli slicer!

I like to consider myself a provocateur of a good time, so I begged the often-shy granddaughter, Beatrice, to play the violin with her father for her grandmother. That year was the first time I was able to get her to play for our guests and it was amazing. She hemmed and hawed, but I even got Matteo to join in to coax Beatrice and her father, Maurizio, to play. They finally agreed.

Before the birthday cake was presented to Nonna, the duet performed a piece from Bach, which brought tears to Nonna's eyes. I don't know why, but several of the family members there had never seen the two exhibit their beautiful talents. I found that odd since my father was an amazing piano player and I cherish the memories of him playing at house parties. I guess that's why I was so persistent in getting them to play.

With the arrival of the birthday cake we sang "Happy Birthday" to Nonna. There was also an out-of-this-world chocolate cake and my *baklava*, making a trifecta dessert you can usually only dream about. There I was, experiencing a special moment across the world, yet feeling like a member of this family in their home. I love this family so much and it was a day I will always remember.

Guests Become Friends

Over the years it's been a common experience to host tour guests and instantly become friends. Many in the Sarasota area have become close friends who have supported me in many ways. I'll always be forever grateful to Michele Stephan who brought her loving family to Tuscany as clients the year after she visited with that first group to support my business. Since that trip, I've had the pleasure to cook with her friends and family, and she has remained a big supporter of my business.

Kimberly Pelyk purchased the *How Italian Food Conquered the World* dinner auction item at a charity gala and, after meeting me, booked a group to tour Sicily to celebrate a significant birthday. Her time in Sicily included dinner with my cousins in Montelepre and a walk along the seashore in Scopello. I remember some sheep and their herding dog visited us on our walk. The little dog with his radio collar had come up to us for a sniff and quickly realized we were friends. The birthday party with her friends in the Sicilian villa was so heartwarming it was impossible not to be friends after that experience. Kimberly is still one of my greatest supporters and has done so many things for me over the years.

There have been so many new friends. Like Pete and Joyce Ronan, whose reply to their children's question about wanting a 50th wedding anniversary party was, "Yes, if you can get Robert to come to Detroit and do the food."

We did just that and my siblings helped out. My sister Roseann helped serve and my brother Joe's band provided the entertainment.

Tom and Susan Ghezzi and Mary Harper and Randy Mikkelson have become wonderful friends, inviting me to many of their parties. I truly enjoyed witnessing Tom's amateur standup comedy performance. This one-time insurance actuary took a standup comedy class at the local comedy club and now has fun with it as a hobby.

Ed and Christine Webler, Joseph Muscatello, Melissa Anderson, and many more are all examples of the amazing gift of friendship I received from hosting them, and sometimes their entire families, in Italy.

There are several more examples of the friendships I have made over the course of this transition. The creation of such friendships was something I did not expect when I made the decision to change careers, but it has been one of the most rewarding aspects of it. I've truly been blessed with these friendships that go far beyond the tour experiences we shared.

Chapter 9

THE LOST YEARS

The COVID-19 pandemic has affected the economy in various industries around the world in quite different ways. For some, it created a boom of new business, creating record years for the home improvement industry, online commerce, companies providing recreational activities and equipment, and even puzzle manufacturers, to name just a few. But for others, like professionals in the tourism industry, our way of making a living was completely devastated because of the lockdowns and the social distancing protocols governments have enacted to slow down the pandemic.

In Italy, it was a disastrous year for all the colleagues with whom I have built my business over the past seven years. I feel so honored to be able to call them colleagues and have been blessed with their friendships and impressed with their work from the start. Unlike the uncertainty I experienced during the banking industry crash, watching the effects of the COVID-19 crisis on my friends and colleagues was more disappointing than financially devastating for me.-

Sarah Wilson-Ferry

I've witnessed so many heartbreaking situations for my friends in the travel industry and not just the professionals I work with in Italy. There is Sarah, a dear friend I watched grow up. My family and hers vacationed in northern Michigan and shared campsites next to each other every year. Through the years, Sarah graduated from college with an undergraduate degree in Hospitality Business and received her MBA. She then established a successful career in the hotel industry.

She did not know at the time the pandemic hit that it would mark the end of a 21-year journey. From banquet server to road warrior and everything in between, Sarah grew so passionate about her work over that time. Research from the firm Tourism Economics and the US Travel Association found that the travel economic footprint in the United States shrank 42 percent in 2021, from $2.6 trillion to $1.5 trillion, a deficit of more than $1 trillion. Sarah got caught in that massive decline and lost her position with one of the largest hoteliers in the world. Through it all, Sarah kept a positive attitude, even after sending out hundreds of resumes and submitting over 200 applications resulting in more than 20 interviews. She finally made the decision to change careers and found an exciting position in the healthcare industry. I'm happy to know she persevered through it all and although she still grieves the loss of the life she once lived and loved in the tourism industry, she is incredibly grateful for all that she learned in those pivotal nine months she was without a job. As she puts it, "We don't know where we will be in a year, but I choose joy and gratitude for all that I have been blessed with!"

I often think of how Sarah kept her good attitude and pressed on even though the odds were against her. She has been an inspiration for me and I'll always try to keep on pressing on when the hard times come along in this volatile business.

Sandra Giusti

One of my Italian colleagues had a life-changing event happen at the beginning of the pandemic. Sandra Giusti had provided our guests with wonderful city tours of Arezzo in Tuscany during the town's jousting games and festivals. She and her husband have been blessed with the birth of their little boy, Lorenzo, during the first strict lockdown Italy had to endure. Before the virus spread, she was prepared to be just a mom for a while. She had planned to take a little break from her job, and start working again with a lot of enthusiasm in the summer since she adores her job as a tour guide. Then the virus and all the necessary restrictions hit. Sandra and her husband lost all their booked tours (they both work as tour guides and tour leaders), which caused them a lot of worries since their baby was expected in a few days.

Then Lorenzo was born, and he was well and healthy! She says, "He made us so happy and we felt we had been blessed with him. What is sad is that neither our parents, nor siblings, nor friends could see Lorenzo until he was two months old, and I couldn't have my mom close to me after childbirth.

"Lorenzo had his first birthday and again we could not see our relatives because of the new restrictions, and I felt sad that, after a year, we still could not let him live a normal life. He just saw loved ones with their masks on and his grandparents could not even kiss him once. But we have to be grateful about everything and we don't want to complain since we're fine and we're not living under the bombs or as refugees."

Luckily, the couple was able to find a little work until Christmas. Sandra worked as a shop assistant in a beautiful toy store, and it was an amazing experience for her. Unfortunately, the position had to be eliminated due to the new restrictions and the store's economic troubles. The couple remains optimistic about the future though, and have been working on planning new tours.

Cristina Amberti

Cristina Amberti is also a tour guide in Tuscany and has provided my company's groups with tours of Siena since the beginning. In 2019, she had received many walking-tour bookings and remained busy from spring until late fall, including November. Cristina had both new and repeat clients booked to explore Tuscany in 2020, which included tours of Siena as the highlight of their trips. Her agenda was full of confirmations and 2020 was going to be one of her best years ever. After a winter break, March usually means the start of the tourist season, but March 2020 held a different plan for everybody.

Cristina lives in the Tuscan countryside and tells me she spent her newfound free time exploring the several outbuildings spread around her property. They are filled with the many things she has collected over the years. There are books, magazines, paintings, pieces of furniture, clothes, and things from her children's childhood, which all had to be sorted with the help of her husband.

They removed a great deal of unnecessary stuff. One of those emptied outbuildings was turned into a gym, which they used during the lockdowns. Cristina said, "Needless to say, I have exercised, cooked, read books, and watched films more than usual."

Cristina also spent her time taking pleasure in nature, tending the many rose, wisteria, and jasmine bushes, as well as the fruit trees that they had planted over the years. They all received extra care during the pandemic year.

In one of our conversations Cristina explained, "In Tuscany roses bloom from April to May depending on the type. Yellow ones are climbing roses or landscape roses and are the first ones to bloom, but the blooming doesn't last for a long time. They are great for two weeks and then nothing until next year, a kind of supreme symbolism of the idea of a garden. In medieval culture, the garden was the allegory of life because it was closed, artificial, and ephemeral."

Cristina's red roses are Seville roses, which are produced by Meilland in France. They have won the ADR German prize as the most resistant roses, which is a great help in maintaining her garden during the cold winter months in Tuscany.

The white flowers in her garden are Aspirin roses commissioned by the Bayer AG to celebrate the 100-year anniversary of Bayer Aspirin. They are very popular among gardeners now because the flowers are decorative and easy to grow. Cristina went on to say, "The color is incredibly elegant and turns from light rose to white. They are ground cover roses."

Cristina gives a fair warning about wisteria: "Be careful where you plant it, because its roots are devastating. They are so strong and able to damage pipes and building foundations. If your Zodiac sign is Pisces, it's your plant. It helps you be more rooted to the earth."

The type of jasmine in Cristina's garden is Trachelospermum Jasminoides. Cristina explained "It's an evergreen whose flowers bloom until June/July and their scent is unforgettable. My garden must be nice-looking but also full of perfumes."

From the summer until mid-October, Italians could travel within the country's boundaries, and wonderful Siena was happily invaded by visitors. Working with Italians instead of English- or French-speaking travelers was a great experience for Cristina. She said with delight, "I even had the chance to lead tours for Sienese and Tuscans; some of them decided to learn in-depth about their region or city for the first time."

I was fortunate to have Cristina as a guest presenter for some of the virtual classes I taught during the lockdowns. Since I could no longer teach in person, I had to develop virtual classes and utilize many of the guides I've worked with over the years. One class was about the pilgrimage in Tuscany, and the guests found learning about all the little towns along the way to Rome fascinating.

Concetta "Cetti" Spoto

Concetta "Cetti" Spoto is a special tour guide in Palermo, Sicily with whom I've been working for the past five years. Cetti was also on the heels of her best year ever since starting her business over 20 years ago. The pandemic turned her life upside-down. The lockdowns made it difficult to live day-to-day life, but she tried to keep her mind busy. Cetti has teamed up with me to create informative classes about Sicily. Although she can't take people around her city and other sites in Sicily in person, she has found a way to help people travel using their imaginations. She wants to organize lessons that help make her island more known. One of my favorite programs is titled, "Discover the Splendors of Norman Sicilian Golden Age." So many of Sicily's treasures were left behind by the Normans from around 1,000 AD to 1,200 AD, that many have been given UNESCO World Heritage designations.

Chiara Rozzi

It was the isolation and inactivity that sparked a new source of creativity for Chiara Rozzi, a tour guide specialist with 25 years' experience in Taormina, Sicily. Chiara's story reflects what is possible when a productive person is forced to stop doing what she is so passionate about. I will let you learn of Chiara's COVID-19 story from her own writings, sent to me a year after the start of the pandemic:

"...for me, the missed season was supposed to be the most incredible and busiest of my career, (that started in 1987 until the beginning of March, 2020). I was wondering how I could succeed in accomplishing all the work I accepted. And almost suddenly all this ferment simply stopped.

"At the very beginning of the pandemic, I was convinced this had to be just for a short while. Never and never, could I imagine that the governments of the whole world could decide and even more incredibly, succeed to close people inside and for such a long time! I still wonder if this really helped to contain the pandemic and if the costs in terms of economy and collective fear was worthwhile.

"Anyway, the first period of lockdown I accepted the situation as it was, despite my disbelief. Staying closed at home was not that bad because, fortunately, I live in an isolated house in the countryside. So that I could enjoy the plants and trees blossoming in my garden and all around, I started to put them in colored compositions on my kitchen table. I also shared this beauty, sending photos of them with WhatsApp to bring hope to my friends.

"I brought this idea from India, the last journey I did in January with a friend. Outside, spring was flourishing and our lives inside were frozen like in a nightmare.

"Reading again books such as *The Plague* by Camus (!!!), *Siddhartha* by Hermann Hesse. Putting order, at last, in my documents, papers, and drawers. Rediscovering forgotten memories, throwing away a lot of old and useless things, cleaning, cooking, getting fat (sigh!!!), regularly taking vitamin D and magnesium, meditating, gardening, attending yoga lessons online, getting massages from my expert daughter, watching movies and serials on Netflix (*Suits*, my favorite...! 9 seasons...!!!) and any kind of funny stories on YouTube, and above all AVOIDING NEWS! Just once a day I'd check the situation of hospitals and realized the problems were not enough beds and healthcare staff and not knowing how to manage this disease. Otherwise, the percentages of ill people compared to the population were objectively not as terrible as the medias wanted to let us think.

"Technology helped me stay in contact with my friends through video calling. Some friends were much more alone than me; at least my youngest daughter, 24 years old, still lives with me. My eldest one works in Germany.

"Some colleagues of mine were so smart and resilient that they were able to recycle themselves working with virtual tours all the time. I felt inadequate in that regard. However, I did turn a short promotional video and put it in my website.

"Summer arrived, and they seemed to reopen again. Almost no work for me, apart from a couple of walking tours in Taormina with Italians, French, and Germans. Was I still able to do my job? Apparently, yes, but did I still feel like doing it? No answer! Better to go to beach, biking at dawn and coming back at 9:30 a.m. before it was too hot, or late in the evening before sunset. Things that I haven't done in decades—no time for such pleasure before.

"Then Autumn arrived, no auspices of work, just cancellations. Money reserves were dwindling...

"So, how to pass another winter without becoming crazy? Chiara, you must find out an Option B! OK, let's start painting watercolors. And there I was, improving my artistic techniques since October, distributing my works as presents among my friends. If I concentrate my mind on drawing and painting, I don't waste time thinking nonsense and being worried. Just here and now.

"But how long can I last with this pandemic? Sometimes it's difficult not to feel lonely, not having physical contact with people for such a long time. We are human beings depending on one another's touch. During the bombing from the war, everyone at least could cling together and later they supported each other by rebuilding the destroyed towns. Unlike those times, this pandemic has separated people and new psychological discomforts are already appearing on the horizon.

"So, one year passed by and it's spring again, we should take stock of the situation. But how long will this last?"

Like Chiara, I too missed the touch and embrace of my friends and family in Italy. I adore how Italians kiss each cheek of the person they greet, male or female. A simple gesture of love for the people in their lives, and it has been almost a year as I write this since I've been able to do just that. I miss Tuscany, and the quiet, beauty-filled walks I would take in the vineyard or hiking up to my friend Candida's house for coffee while my guests toured for the day. I also miss walking up the mountain to my cousin Vita's summer villa in Sicily and helping myself to a fig or two from a roadside tree along the way. The food, the wine, and the sights are all the obvious things one would miss about Italy, but for me what I miss the most are the smiles on my friends' and family members' faces as we embrace after a long absence.

Chapter 10:

"YOU'RE TAKING ME TO PUGLIA THIS YEAR, RIGHT?"

There is one friend I met during my career transition I haven't mentioned yet. His name is Charles Matthew Webster, Jr. We met on the pickleball court at The Center on Anna Maria Island, Florida. Meeting Chuck was a gift.

When we met, he asked me, "What do you do?"

"I have a small travel company that specializes in tours to Italy," I replied.

After listening for about two minutes, Chuck said, "Put me down for a reservation for your next tour." This was about eight months out from our tour season, though it isn't unusual for people to have that kind of response. If I had booked a guest every time I got that sort of response, I would have been booked out for the next ten years. But the reality is that life gets in the way of doing the things we want to do.

So, I went to the lobby and grabbed one of my rack cards to give him. I provided Italian cultural and cooking classes at The Center so they allowed me to place my cards in the lobby. After giving him the card, he instructed me to contact his assistant at his office and set everything up.

Chuck ended up coming to Tuscany in 2019 and had a wonderful experience, which for me was a huge compliment since he is a world-class traveler and has been on many vacations, including several in Italy. To have his approval meant a great deal to me. However, it goes much further than that. During one of our conversations, I mentioned that I needed a place to live back home before I could go to Italy in 2020 to apply for my Italian citizenship. Finding a temporary place to live during the high season (fall and winter) in Sarasota, Florida, isn't an easy task, but without batting an eye, Chuck offered his newly renovated home on Anna Maria for the entire season. He hadn't even stayed in the home yet since its renovation and didn't even let me pay for the cleaning service for the duration of my stay there.

Little did I know at the time just how important this gift would be. During my stay, COVID-19 totally devastated my business, and I would not earn an income for the following two years. I not only got to stay in a beautiful, newly renovated home right on the water facing Tampa Bay, but I didn't have housing expenses to worry about just before a huge economic loss due to the pandemic. I had only known this kind and generous man for less than a year, yet he opened his home to me without giving it a second thought. Ending my story of this new friendship here would still make it an exceptional story, but it's not the end. You see, after not doing what I love for two years, it was Chuck who was so persistent in getting me to return to work and take him to Italy.

In May of 2021, due to the uncertainty of the pandemic, I canceled all my scheduled tours that had been planned for that fall. I was a bit depressed. But it was Chuck who said, "You're taking me to Puglia this year, right?"

It didn't matter what the risks of travel could be, he was hellbent on getting back to Italy no matter what, and he wanted me to make that happen.

To have the support of this man has been an absolute gift, and after all the loss and disappointments month after month during the pandemic, it was just what I needed to get back to work. And just like before, I contacted Ann, his wonderful assistant, and we planned an incredible trip to Puglia as well as a week on the Amalfi Coast for him and his cousin Guy and his wife, Lori, and his great friend of 20 years, RC, and his wife, Heather.

The anticipation for the trip was intense and stressful. It seemed like every day there was something changing about international travel requirements. There was also the concern that a positive COVID test could prevent me or one or more of my guests from traveling—or returning, for that matter. Given the level of stress, I was reaffirmed that I had made the right decision to cancel my tours, except Chuck's. And although it was a big financial loss and another heavy disappointment, it was the right thing to do. When guests take my tour, everything needs to be perfect, and the uncertainty of the situation couldn't guarantee that.

Our trip started in Sorrento; however, flights were still unpredictable at that time. Without warning, Chuck's flight was canceled, and the airlines didn't make it easy for him to find another flight. However, he still arrived the next day and I was at the airport to greet him. Miraculously, it was the only glitch on the entire trip.

The Roman ruins of Herculaneum.

If ever there were a time to visit Italy, it was in 2021. The streets of Amalfi and Sorrento, normally packed with people, were much less populated during our stay. Capri was also so much more enjoyable without the heavy crowds. We visited many of my favorite spots like Paestum, Sorrento, Herculaneum, and the Blue Grotto on Capri.

If you've ever wanted to see an example of what a Roman town looked like in 79 A.D., then you should plan a visit to Herculaneum. This Roman vacation seaport was covered by a hot lava and mud mixture, instead of the ash that covered Pompeii, which preserved many of the homes in this city of more than 2,000 people. The mainly pyroclastic material that covered Herculaneum carbonized and preserved the wood in roofs, beds, and doors, as well as other organic-based materials such as food and papyrus. It was an incredible sight to see with our tour guide and just a handful of other tourists there. The trip was filled with food and wine and on our Puglia leg of the tour, we even got to pick grapes at the Mazzone Winery and make cheese at a picturesque family farm. There were other added visits to Matera and Tivoli, and again, there were small crowds and few Americans as well.

Making cheese in Puglia.

To me, Matera is an amazing example of what human society was like in the earliest times in Europe. This UNESCO-designated city is a maze of stone and manmade structures that have been occupied for over 10,000 years. The Sasso, which means stone in Italian, are the neighborhoods that make up the core of the city. There are two of them—Sasso Caveoso (built into the rock caves) and Sasso Barisano (built on top of the rock). It was in the early 1950s that the Italian government used forced eviction to relocate most of the population of the Sassi to new public housing in the developing modern city. This was part of a policy to clear the extreme poverty in the area which made Matera (at the time) the disgrace of Italy.

Today the city has been revitalized. In the 1980s the government sought to create an environment that is more tourism-oriented, and it has promoted the Sassi as a picturesque tourist attraction, with the aid of the Italian government and its UNESCO designation. Now there are many thriving businesses, pubs, and hotels there, and the city is among the fastest-growing in southern Italy. There have also been a few movies filmed there, including a James Bond movie in 2019, bringing this jewel to the attention of the world.

Tivoli is also a special place for me. I love water, and there the water dances all around you in the gardens of the Villa d'Este. This 16th-century villa is famous for its numerous beautiful fountains cascading through the terraced hillsides. It is also a museum and another listed UNESCO World Heritage Site which my guests were able to see in 2021. The fountains range from small animal heads that water trickles gently from to the grand fountains in the heart of the garden that shoot water at least 30 feet into the air. This graceful and glorious site was all engineered using gravity, not pumps.

Hadrian's Villa in Tivoli.

I'm so grateful and very fortunate to have had clients, and now friends, to share these amazing experiences with.

That tour was the one and only tour in 2021 but it was a success that could not have been more meaningful to me. An authentic experience with a small group is what many post-pandemic travelers will be looking for, and that is exactly what I plan to provide for them.

When the time came for my guests to return home and I had dropped them at the Rome airport, I traveled on to Florence to visit some friends. My first stop was at Antonella and Luigi's where I was finally introduced to not just little Luigi, who had been born just before the lockdown, but also to their new bambino, Giulio, who was born just a few months before I arrived. The joy of seeing both Antonella and Luigi was already overwhelming, but to also see their growing family was truly endearing. I even got to babysit Giulio while mommy went to the preschool to pick up Luigi.

The next day Antonella, Giulio, and I went to Florence to have lunch at Luigi's restaurant. It was thrilling to be back in my beloved Florence and eat at Luigi's like I had done so many times before. This nostalgic time made me appreciate the incredible journey I've been on even more. One of Antonella's music associates, Fabrizio, happened to be there as well, and he treated me to my own private piano concert inside the restaurant.

From Florence, I traveled south to San Casciano for the pleasure of having my friend Candida prepare dinner for me and a few of my friends. Before I got there, I stopped by the villa to see Loredana. True to form, over the pandemic she had worked on the house to install new handcrafted wood windows throughout, an indoor dining hall with a laundry room behind it, and other improvements. It was a typically stunning fall day in Tuscany, with the sky so clear that the sun just permeates the soul. It was so emotionally heart-warming to see my friend and all the improvements and love she had continued to put into the villa.

For dinner, Candida invited her friend and my chef, Sandra, whom I regularly hire for our Tuscany tours. Sandra had come all the way down from Venice for the occasion. There were also Loredana; Elena, my Tuscan tour guide, and her friend Barbara; along with a new friend I had recently made in Lucca, Tanja. Elena has been my guide in Tuscany since the beginning, with good reason. She is simply the best! She is so good at what she does, and her love of art really captivates our guests when they visit Florence, the most beautiful art-filled city in the world. I also love it when she takes us into the countryside to visit wine and cheese farms or into San Gimignano, a most enchanting walled town that has several medieval towers still standing today.

Imagine yourself in a country farmhouse in Tuscany surrounded by vineyards in front of an open hearth and a blazing fire warming the dining area on a cool autumn evening. This dining room, once the kitchen of this 300-year-old house, had a hearth that functioned as the oven where meals and breads were made for hundreds of years. The table was set with a beautiful assortment of china and tableware Candida had artfully displayed. That was exactly the setting I experienced during this most festive reunion.

While viewing all the hats and hat molds that decorate Candida's living room, our guests enjoyed an aperitivo. Then we were treated to a delicious meal of lasagna stuffed with mouth-watering cheeses, lamb from her own stock, and an assortment of in-season vegetables. The lamb was roasted, and its preparation was an all-day process, cooking over four hours on very low heat. She did this in a cast iron oven with a gentle wood fire. The recipe includes olive oil, onion, shallots, garlic, sage, rosemary, carrot, parsley, celery, basil, marjoram, thyme, lemon rind, oregano, bay leaf, and as Candida puts it "rivers of red wine." Her effort was a great success.

The meal finished with a chocolate torta Candida had prepared earlier that day along with the chocolates I had purchased in Lucca as a reunion gift. I couldn't have dreamed of a more joyous occasion; it made me think of all the great times we've shared with our guests in Candida's home and the many more we will have in the coming years.

From San Casciano, I was off to Magenta, near Milan, to see Silvia and her family. Four years had passed since I had last seen them, and we had planned a special celebration for Gabriele's 60th birthday. Since our last meeting, Gianni, Silvia's brother, had bought a 1400cc 2010 Fatboy Harley Davidson in mint condition, which he proudly showed me in the garage.

In the morning we went to one of our favorite coffee stops at Pasticceria Porta, which is a delectable dolce shop filled with handmade candies and chocolates. The owner, Adriano Porta, is always there and it's normal for him and Silvia to engage in an Italian political faceoff over the current issues facing the town and general politics. One year Adriano had asked me if I liked Donald Trump, and not thinking of anything else to say, I politely replied, "I like his taste in women."

After coffee we took a walk to Silvia's close friend Carlo's delicatessen in town, *Salumeria di Ronzio Carlo*, to pick up some tasty lunch meats. The salumeria has been in business since 1966 and received the "Negozio Storico," which is a designated acknowledgment by the Region of Lombardia that Salumeria di Ronzio Carlo is an historic business in the region.

While there, he gave me another bottle of antique red wine from the region to go along with the two he had given me four years prior. You can't drink the stuff—well, you can, but it might go better as a salad dressing ingredient. However, the unopened bottles are collectable for their historic value, and I like the old labels. Gabriele looked up the bottle he gave me on the web, and it was selling for about 50 euros.

It's always so much fun visiting these wonderful stores because the experience is rarely replicated in the U.S., and almost impossible in Sarasota. We do have Morton's Gourmet Market in Sarasota, owned by my dear friend Eddie Morton and his son Todd, which has had family ownership for more than 50 years. But you would need to go all the way to Mazzaro's Italian Market in St. Petersburg to get the same vibe as being in Italy. Returning to Italy in 2021 was just what my heart needed after such a long time away from my Italian family and the land I have come to love. It felt great to be back again.

Chapter 11

A CHANCE TO WANDER IN ITALY AGAIN

Driving in my Renault (a French car, please forgive me), I started a trip in the north at Lake Garda and drove south along the beautiful eastern coastline all the way to Sicily. It had been so long since a simple trip wandering through Italy was possible that the idea of touring some off-the-beaten-path places sounded very appealing. Plus, it would allow me to do some research along the way. Mixing some work with a lot of pleasure, I made my way down the Adriatic coast as slowly as possible to see some places I'd never seen and take in as much of this beautiful country as possible.

After a visit to San Casciano, it was time for me to get back to work (if that is what you want to call it), traveling up to Riva del Garda to meet with my tour guide, Claudia, to button down our Dolomites tour for the coming year. This tour had been sold out for its debut in 2020, but like so many other disappointments due to the pandemic,

Biotopo Lago (lake) di Toblino.

it had to be postponed. But things truly worked out for the better, because I didn't have Claudia managing the program in 2020. Now that she's on board, she's lined up a wonderful chalet our guests will absolutely love for the coming year. Claudia is a seasoned tour guide and operator and our working relationship started during the pandemic when I had utilized her skills to present a virtual program for an adult enrichment class.

Claudia scheduled two full days of visiting villas and other places to consider booking for our tightened Dolomites tour. We want to make it a magical experience. The Dolomite Mountains tour will provide premium accommodations with two nights in the gorgeous lake town of Bardolino and a week in Selva di Val Gardena. It includes a personal chef in the chalet, and features a stop in Verona with an excursion to Sirmione by boat, and the mountain towns of Bolzano, Merano, Caldaro, Selva di Val Gardena, and Ortisei by private van. All of this with the enchantment of the Dolomites.

But my personal tour started in Riva del Garda, at the northern tip of Lake Garda, to be close to where Claudia lives. What a lovely place to set up a three-night base camp—Riva has a shoreline filled with beautiful places to stay and a lively historical city center. Although I was there in October, the town was still active, with its many nice places for dining. Lake Garda is one of my favorite places to visit and if it were summertime, I would not have been able to resist renting a boat. There is something truly magical about a lake outing on a sunny day with the mountains as a backdrop.

For the work at hand though, the weather was perfect. It provided us a clear view of the massive mountains as the sun shone on the rock, creating an array of colors that were a feast for the eyes. Having the great pleasure of driving thousands of miles up, down, and all around Italy, I can honestly proclaim that this part of Italy is one of the most beautiful places you can visit.

We visited the towns of Merano, Selva di Val Gardena, and Bolzano and had a 10 a.m. beer at The Hopfen & Co. in Bolzano, a tavern brewery that can be relied on for good food, good beer, and a good mood. Many people don't realize that this part of Italy was part of Austria before the First World War. After the war, in 1919, the region was transferred to Italy in the Treaty of Saint-Germain-en-Laye.

The Assumption of Our Lady Cathedral in Bolzano.

Trentino-Alto Adige is one of five regions that still has its own political autonomy along with Friuli-Venezia Giulia, Sardinia, Sicily, and Val d'Aosta. They are still part of Italy, but have more local control of taxes, local laws, and how funds are spent. In Trentino-Alto Adige, about 30 percent of the population speaks German, and the food and beverages are very Bavarian. Claudia explained to me that during the First World War, Italian-speaking citizens living in Trentino, like her grandfather, had to fight against other Italians. It must have been much like our Civil War, with some family members living on each side of the border fighting against each other.

Driving up 7,346 feet, to the Passo Pordoi, the view was spectacular. It is the highest surface road pass in the Dolomites. Because it was a clear day, we could see Sassolungo and the Sella group of mountains, and even the Marmolada Glacier. In this area, with its mountains and *malgas* (mountain pastures/meadows) providing the grass to feed the cows in the spring, some of the most famous cheeses in the world are produced here. As the summer progresses, the cows graze farther up, which is why the cheeses have different flavors depending on the time of year. This UNESCO World Heritage site is also a downhill skiers' paradise, with many slopes around the mountain creating some of the best skiing in the world.

The next day, after visiting a beautiful country chalet, we visited Merano to do a walking tour of the sprawling and charming town. For lunch, I had Wiener schnitzel and potatoes, and a massive fresh baked pretzel at Forsterbräu Meran Ristorante Birreria, which I washed down with a pint of Forst Heller Bock. I was amazed I was still in Italy. The food was very German and the rather large brewery and restaurant managed to deliver a delicious meal.

Robert enjoying a beer and pretzel at Forsterbräu Meran restaurant, Merano.

If you visit Merano, make time to take in the unique nature, culture, and art at the Gardens of Trauttmansdorff Castle. There are 80 different garden landscapes covering almost 30 acres, providing visitors with a wide array of experience stations, themed gardens, artist pavilions, and animal life. It's been awarded the title of "Italy's Most Beautiful Garden" and the "International Garden of the Year in 2013."

After saying goodbye to Claudia, I started the next phase of our tour with my dear friend Saylor. I wanted to research places to possibly take travelers who have less interest in the more recognized tourist sites of Italy, like Rome, Florence, Venice, and Amalfi Coast. I want to call the tour "The Other Italy," and to include less-known regions like Ancona and Puglia.

The city of Ancona is the capital of the region of Le Marche—a region I had never spent time in, but I had read much about its beauty and food. Our accommodations were at the Seebay Hotel, located in the Bay of Portonovo and surrounded by a wonderful scenic park. With only two nights for our stay, we had to make the most of our daily excursions.

The first day included trips to Ancona, Osimo, Loreto, and Recanati. Ancona is too big of a city to try to see in just a few hours so I still want to return with more time and hire a local guide to do it justice. We were, however, able to take a pleasant walk along Ancona Harbor, which is one of the most important ports in the Adriatic Sea for passenger travel, fishing, and cargo. We also viewed the Marina Dorica, with its array of fishing and sailing boats, yachts, and restaurants.

At the other end of the marina is the Arch of Trajan, a majestic monument built in the second century in honor of Emperor Trajan, who had helped develop and defend the city during the Roman Empire. Unfortunately, we didn't have time to visit its museums, Roman amphitheater, beach, or caves. But we were able to enjoy the fresh seafood that night with a delicious dinner of grilled octopus and some seasonal pumpkin tortellini. The waiter and chef were so accommodating and prepared our octopus just the way we wanted it.

Our next stop was Jesi, with its city walls among the best-preserved in the Marche region. It is the birthplace of one of my favorite characters from Italy's past, Frederick II. The wall was originally constructed in medieval times (13th–14th centuries) which probably followed and possibly extended the old Roman tract. In the Piazza Federico II, the Frederick II Museum is in the Palazzo Ghislieri. In front of the museum in the piazza is a painted outline of the location of the tent where the Holy Roman Emperor was born. On December 26, 1194, Empress Constance, having arrived at Jesi from Piacenza, gave birth to Frederick-Roger, named after his maternal and paternal grandfathers. Later in his life, Frederick II was particularly attached to his city of birth.

Legend has it his mother gave birth in a tent erected in the square in front of the cathedral to dispel every doubt of his legitimacy as heir. The advanced age of his mother, who was 40 at the time, justifies the legend, along with the fact that she had been unable to provide Henry VI with an heir during the previous eight years of marriage. Their decision to stay in Jesi was certainly influenced by the city's loyalty to the Imperial cause; the city had already hosted the Emperor and Empress for several weeks in 1186.

The museum offers visitors a voyage across time into the life of Frederick II with a multimedia, multisensorial experience, showcasing a piece of history that changed the fate of the world. There aren't many artifacts there, but the presentation is a really good depiction of the emperor's life, done in an engaging and captivating way.

The foundation of the emperor's success had been the joining of the two major powers of the time: the Swabian dynasty and the Kingdom of Sicily. The emperor compared Jesi to Bethlehem, defining it as "our Bethlehem," and urged the city to ally itself to the Imperial cause. The use of the letter "J" in the city's name is unusual, since the letter "J" isn't in the Italian alphabet. It's a reference to Jesus, so the implications of it becoming the birthplace of Frederick II were profound.

Jesi is also the birthplace of the famous composer, Giovanni Battista Pergolesi. The Teatro G.B. Pergolesi is a tribute to him as well as Gaspare Spontini, who was born in nearby Malotati, and is credited with creating more than 20 operas. He became an important figure in French opera as well.

Jesi is a beautiful town to explore and wander through places like the Planettiana Municipal Library, which is located in the 15th-century Palazzo della Signoria, one of the city's most magnificent Renaissance buildings. It has the Clementine Arch (1734) on one end and a small park on the other, giving visitors a stunning panoramic view of the eastern Italian countryside.

Trying to make the most of our time, but still wanting to take in the flavor of the Marche region, we visited the small town of Maiolati Spontini next. There, the Santo Stefano di Maiolati Spontini church has an organ loft above the entrance playing music. In keeping with the theme, the entryway's decorated wood carvings depict cherubs playing musical instruments.

The small town of Serra San Quirico, perched on a large hill, offers a rigorous walk through the park to reach the small medieval tower at the peak. It rewards visitors and hikers with a magical view of the countryside. It was especially beautiful to see that day because of the puffy white clouds rolling in below the hill.

By the time we reached the city of Fabiano, the daylight was fleeting. However, a massive street festival was coming to life, which gave us the opportunity to purchase some delicious local cheeses, cured meats, and flavorful olives. This turned the back section of my car into a bountiful food pantry. On our drive back to the hotel, Saylor read some articles about the town and we learned that it is known for its paper industry and the production of the highest quality paper. I wished we had had more time to

A medieval tower in the small town of Serra San Quirico.

visit Fabiano. I will be sure to return some day to give it the attention it deserves.

Clear blue sky greeted us the next morning on our way to Osimo.
The town hall there has an interesting collection of decapitated
Roman sculptures, which people refer to as "the Headless Statues,"
as well as other Roman artifacts on display through the hallway and

courtyard. Osimo is a major Templar site, with documents dating back to 1187, confirming it to be one of the most important Templar locations in the Marche region.

We also visited the Cattedrale San Leopardo. The white stone of the cathedral reflected brightly in the sun and inside, a stone arch and rosette window make it a mesmerizing sight to see. Built in 1191, the church is one of the most beautiful examples of Romanesque-Gothic architecture in the region. The altar within is decorated with frescoes and a beautifully illustrated Bible.

If you ever visit Osimo, I highly recommend its public garden dedicated to Camillo Acqua, a biologist and naturalist. The

These headless statues gave the city of Osimo its nickname
"City of the Headless."

panoramic view from my vantage point was breathtaking on that clear and bright day. Osimo is another town that warrants a longer visit from me. I would like to visit the series of caves there, filled with enigmatic medieval engravings connected to initiation rituals and symbols of the Templar.

Next stop, Loreto. It is a special place because it is the location of the Sanctuary of the Holy House of Loreto, where beneath the large dome the Holy House of Nazareth is preserved. This is the house where Jesus is to have lived and where the Virgin Mary grew up. Recent research has verified the origins of the bricks of the house, and the hypothesis is that the house was carried by the Angeli family on board a ship to the hills of Loreto. It has been one of the main pilgrimage destinations in the world since the beginning of the 14th century. Kings, queens, cardinals, and more than 50 popes have

Sanctuary of the Holy House of Loreto.

come to visit the Holy House. Regardless of one's faith, the mere fact that these devout people brought back each brick of this house from thousands of miles away, a thousand years ago, is truly remarkable. It was a serene experience walking through the house and thinking of the communal effort it took to bring it to this location.

The famous Piazza della Madonna is the artistic and religious center of Loreto and includes the Maggiore Fountain, the Statue of Pope Sixtus V, the Apostolic Palace, the bell tower, and the imposing Basilica. There street artists reproduce famous religious paintings using simple colored chalk in front of the Basilica.

A stunning view of a long stretch of the Riviera can be seen from Loreto. On your walk to see the view, you can visit a peaceful and serene World War II military cemetery for the 2nd Polish Corps, where 1,090 officers and soldiers were buried during the war.

Next, we visited Recanati, known for being the homeland of the famous tenor Beniamino Gigli. It is also the home of the illustrious poet Giacomo Leopardi, one of the principals of literary romanticism and considered the greatest Italian poet of the 19th century. Leopardi's impact on the town is everywhere, from the piazza named after him that holds a monument in his honor to a national study center to promote the study of his works. There is also the Palazzo Leopardi, which houses a library of more than 25,000 volumes to which he had dedicated his childhood to study.

Like our other stops, Recanati was too brief, as was the quick picnic on the beach in Civitanova Marche, which I imagine is full of sunseekers and bathers during the summer months. The cool October air kept the crowds away, but the bright blue sky provided a beautiful backdrop for enjoying our meal.

The big prize of the day was the town of Ascoli Piceno. I had read much about the famous fried stuffed olives the town is known for, which I was excited to try. What I didn't know about was the classic old-fashion café Meletti, where locals go to enjoy an aperitivo, anisette, gelato, and other after-dinner treats. Much of the décor is original, from the wood bar to the iron liberty-style decorative columns. The staff was courteous, and we had the most delightful young waiter who took such pride in his work. Here, again, you can find the most satisfying experiences off the beaten path at half the cost of places like Venice.

Anisetta Meletti in Ascoli Piceno was owned by Silvio Meletti, an artisan who perfected an anise-based liquor.

The region of Le Marche is beautiful and the food—from seafood to the famous *olive all'ascolana* (stuffed fried olives)—makes happy hour even happier! One of the things I love about Italy is that each place has its own special foods, and discovering them in person brings great joy to my experience of traveling there. Le Marche is such a place and it will make you want to return as well.

There was a long drive ahead from Ascoli Piceno to the small fishing and beach town of Peschici, in the Gargano National Park sub-region of Puglia. Gargano, the so-called "spur" in the heel of Italy's boot, is unspoiled except for a few seaside resort towns. Its forest is one of the most scenic in all of Italy and its dramatic coastlines of white limestone cliffs are dreamy. In summer, you could easily spend a week here to take in the water as well as the sights. I continue to marvel at the food in Gargano; we didn't even need to leave our hotel because our innkeeper prepared the freshest seafood we'd had yet.

The attractions I remember most vividly on this trip included: Vieste, a fun beach town perfect for wandering; the Foresta Umbra; Peschici, the location of our castle hotel; and Vico del Gargano, a small village off the beaten path. And Monte Sant'Angelo, the location of a UNESCO World Heritage site. I can envision creating a tour focused on these places but with more ambition and energy. It could include activities such as a bike tour through the forest trails, a swim in the beautiful water, and a hike to check out the spectacular views of the cliffs and sea.

In the town of Monte Sant'Angelo is the Sanctuary of San Michele (St. Michael). It is the oldest shrine in Western Europe dedicated to Archangel Michael. In 2011, it became a UNESCO World Heritage Site. It was designated as one of seven Places of Power in the history of the Longobards, a Germanic people who controlled the Lombard region from 568 to 774 A.D. This cave church (a Rupestrian church) is a truly moving experience regardless of your faith; it was an emotional stop for me.

The thought of people gathering underground out of fear of persecution thousands of years ago at this very spot to pray to God, gave me a rush of hope. After taking a moment to immerse myself in the energy of the site, I went to the gift shop and purchased a battery-operated candle and placed it on the altar to ask God for St. Michael's protection for a loved one. When I walked back to the pew I sat in the row behind Saylor and rested my head on her shoulder and just started to cry deeply. It was as if being in the cave church helped me release the fear and sadness I didn't realize I'd been holding.

The ancient cave church; the Sanctuary of St. Michael in Monte Sant'Angelo, Puglia.

Above: The wall of the castle of Monte Sant'Angelo.
Below: Pane di Matera, the ancient bread in the region of Basilicata.

The kitchen area of a typical cave home in Matera.

The Gargano peninsula also has islands and sea caves to explore during the summer. All this, plus seafood as fresh as you can get, makes this part of Puglia a perfect place to discover and roam. Puglia is known for its farming, particularly its olive groves, and the land is flat, so the Gargano peninsula is a wonderful diversion for travelers seeking an outdoor adventure as well as wanting to enjoy the culinary treasures of the region.

While nearby I had to return to Matera to pick up a handcrafted leather bag made by a craftsman there and meet a new tour guide, Stella. I would like to include Matera on private tours for my future guests because it educates the visitor about the historical poverty of the south and a community's ability to create something truly special from that history. So of course, having a relationship with a knowledgeable guide like Stella is very important.

Finally, it was time to get on the car ferry and cross the Strait of Messina to Sicily. There I would be spending the month of November with my family in Montelepre. Having the freedom to spend a whole month with my cousins was a blessing. In my experience, if you haven't been to Sicily, you haven't completely been to Italy.

Chapter 12
COMPLETING THE CIRCLE

Freedom to wander has given me the opportunity to not only visit the place where my family came from, but also the possibility of regaining Italian citizenship that my grandfather had given up more than 100 years earlier when he became an American citizen.

The next phase of my life is to begin the process of becoming a dual citizen through my grandfather, since he was still an Italian citizen at the time of my father's birth. This qualifies me to become an Italian citizen and hopefully, if all goes well, it will complete my journey to reconnect with my roots.

My grandfather left Sicily to find new opportunities and a way to build a better life in America, and I am proof of his success. I did just the opposite, coming to Italy not just for economic opportunity but to reconnect my soul with the land and my family in this beautiful country.

My connection to my new Sicilian family has been a priceless gift, filling my heart with joy and love as a result of their presence in my life. I like to believe I have done the same for them in some small way. This year I had the opportunity to bring a little of my American culture into their lives by providing them with the experience of the quintessential American holiday of Thanksgiving.

Thanksgiving Day Dinner with my Sicilian Family

After the two-year separation due to the pandemic, this return trip was a very special time for me. I wanted to take the opportunity to celebrate in a grand way. I realized I'd be spending Thanksgiving away from the people with whom I normally share holidays, but I also held a deep sense of gratitude for the people I *would* be seeing. I decided I would give thanks for the recent years with my Montelepre family by treating them to an American Thanksgiving Day feast.

It wasn't the easiest task to complete in this little Sicilian town. Whole turkeys aren't something you can find easily, and I didn't think to have fresh cranberries shipped to me from home. However, my cousin, Vitanna, oversaw finding the bird. She turned to Giuseppe, the local butcher. He couldn't find a turkey large enough for our party of 22 cousins and friends, but did find us two 13-pound female "*tacchine*." One went into my oven and the other into Vitanna's.

The cranberries had to come out of a can, since all I could find was Ocean Spray cranberry sauce at a store called The American Store in Palermo. The store had a very enthusiastic owner who said it was the first such store in Sicily, and the second in all of Italy. It's filled with all the processed junk food from America ranging from Doritos to candies, and pancake mix to Twinkies. I found the cranberry sauce and filled my shopping bag with candies like Pop

Preparing the *tacchino* (turkey) for Thanksgiving dinner.

Rocks, Sour Patch gummies, and Warheads (the so-called sourest candy in the world) to give to my youngest cousins as a treat.

The turkeys were fresh, but their shape was much different than the American birds I'm familiar with. Their breasts weren't the exaggerated, water-injected meat sold to American consumers at low prices just to get shoppers into stores. This difference created an unforeseen challenge. An American bird has plenty of moisture, so the stuffing doesn't need to contribute anything except flavor. For these birds however, since I didn't add enough broth to the stuffing (to make up for that lost moisture) it turned out pretty dry, also I

Thanksgiving Day turkey in Montelepre, Sicily.

had to keep adding water to the drippings throughout the cooking process so the meat would stay tender and the bottom drippings wouldn't burn.

I also didn't account for siesta (nap time between 1:00 p.m.–4:00 p.m.) and it was lucky I called Vitanna at 5:00 p.m. to check on how she was progressing with her bird. I had prepared the birds in the morning and brought one to her to start cooking that afternoon. I must have woken her, since it sounded like they were scrambling to get the turkey in the oven. Italians don't eat dinner until 9:00 p.m., so we actually had plenty of time and the results were incredible. They ended up being the best turkeys I have ever prepared. The white meat was just as juicy and tasty as the dark meat, and the gravy was full of flavor.

Even though it isn't a traditional American dish to serve, I couldn't resist making fresh pasta for the occasion and served it with a creamy pistachio sauce. The menu also included my personal caponata recipe (a relish of chopped eggplant and assorted vegetables) and, of course, Luciana's *tiramisù*. However, in keeping with tradition, I did make a pumpkin pie with fresh pumpkin and real whipped cream.

The boys looked with curiosity when I pulled the turkey out of the oven, since they had never seen a turkey cooked this way before. As I carved the turkey, Roberto dropped the succulent chunks of white meat into his mouth before it was even served, and Emanuele loved the turkey gravy. There were some skeptical looks as I dug out the stuffing from the center of the cooked turkeys, but overall, the dinner guests loved their first Thanksgiving Day meal. It was such a grand time having my cousin, Guido, by my side helping me cook. Guido is a master farmer, and he had gifted me a bottle of his hot pepper sauce, which I put on the potato dish his wife had made. Just a few drops were all I needed since this stuff was extremely spicy. I felt so much joy seeing the smiles on my family's faces as I shared my cultural tradition with them.

The decision to take the risk to change my life just keeps on rewarding my soul in so many ways. The following month after I returned to the U.S., my cousin Giovanna sent me a wonderful greeting on my birthday. It roughly translates to "Happy Birthday to our dear cousin, who revolutionized our cousinhood and allows us to reunite even more. Good blood doesn't lie."

My decision to find my Italian family at nearly 50 years old resulted in being reborn into a loving family more than 3,000 miles away and launched my new career in travel. Even after experiencing a worldwide pandemic that sidelined my business for two years, it's hard not to have a smile on my face when I think about the future. The ability to share this Italian experience with guests and my goal of gaining my Italian citizenship keep my passion alive.

Montelepre is the place where my family can be traced back to the 1680s. It's where hundreds of years and many generations passed before my grandfather boarded that steamship to change the course of history for me, my family, and the lives of my American cousins. It's the place that was calling me to visit after a very dark period in my life and it changed my life in ways I never could have imagined at the time.

Having the freedom to wander is not just a means to earn a living, it is how I fill my soul with love and meaning.

ROBERT'S RECIPES

Throughout this book I have listed a smattering of my personal favorite recipes as well as those of our guest favorites. I am pleased to share them with you now. I hope you enjoy them and share them with friends and family. Food is life!

Buon appetito!

—Robert

Sfince di Prescia

This dessert, originating in Montelepre, Sicily, was the first recipe I learned from my cousin Vita, who remembers making this fried flour dough dessert with her grandmother. The Sicilian word *prescia* means hurry because the dough must be hot when you roll it on the wooden pasta board.

Ingredients:

8⅓ cups (1 k) flour
4 cups (1 L) milk
4 cups (1 L) water
3 tbsp. (42.5 g) oil
½ cup (113.4 g) sugar
Pinch of saffron (125 mg)
Oil for deep frying (enough for the dough to float)
1 tbsp. (14.3 g) cinnamon
¼ cup (50 g) sugar

Directions:

In a large bowl, mix the first six ingredients. Cook and quickly stir the mixture over a hot stove. Next, dump the warm dough onto a wooden cutting board and using your hands, roll into foot-long ropes. Cut ropes into smaller, 3-inch pieces (7.6 cm) and twist into an "awareness-ribbon" shape. Drop the formed dough into hot cooking oil and cook until golden brown. Then toss into a bowl of sugar and cinnamon mixture to coat the outside.

Pistachio Cream Sauce

This pistachio cream sauce is simple but does need a little attention when stirring to prevent the cream and cheese from scorching.

Ingredients:

5 tbsp. (70 g) of your best olive oil

½ medium white onion, chopped

¼ lb. (113 g) pancetta (cut into ¼-inch cubes)

¼ cup (36 g) unsalted pistachio nuts, ground coarsely

1 cup (128 g) heavy cream

½ cup (60 g) Parmigiano-Reggiano cheese, grated

Cooked pasta water as needed (1-2 ladles)

Crushed red pepper flakes (optional)

Salt and pepper, to taste

Directions:

Heat oil in a medium sauté pan. Sauté onions with a little salt and *pancetta* until onions are translucent (not caramelized) on medium heat. Add pistachios and, if needed, more olive oil to lightly coat. Cook for about a minute; the pistachios should not change color. Add cream until heated throughout. Add grated Parmigiano-Reggiano cheese, stirring constantly with a whisk, so as not to burn. Stir in a ladle or two of cooked pasta water, red pepper flakes if desired, and salt and pepper to taste.

Saltimbocca alla Romana

This is a classic Roman veal dish. The fresh sage makes the flavors do just what Saltimbocca means: "Jump in the mouth!"

Ingredients:

- 6 veal medallions
- 1-2 fresh sage leaves per medallion
- 6 slices of cheese (optional)
- 6 slices of Prosciutto
- Salt and pepper to taste
- ¼ cup (32 g) flour
- 2 tbsp. (26 g) olive oil
- 2 tbsp. (28.4 g) butter
- ⅛ cup (30 mL) white wine
- Juice from one lemon (2-3 tbsp.) (29-43 g)

Directions:

Place the sage leaf on the meat and then the cheese (optional) and the prosciutto; use a toothpick to keep them in place while cooking. Salt and pepper the veal side and dredge that side in flour. Grill on the stove in olive oil and butter, first the floured side, and then the other side. When the veal is almost cooked, add white wine and lemon juice, cook until the alcohol burns off, and deglaze the pan for the sauce, using a wooden spoon to scrape the pan. Remove the meat and stir in more flour if needed to thicken the sauce, and then serve on top.

Eggplant Rollatini

This eggplant dish was made by Luciana and me the day before our gathering.

Ingredients:

1 large eggplant, peeled and cut lengthwise into ¼-inch (6.35 mm) slices

½ cup (68 g) flour

1 egg, add a little milk and beat

1 cup (119 g) Italian-seasoned, fine breadcrumbs

¼ cup (54 g) frying oil

1 cup (250 g) ricotta cheese

1½ cups (337 g) plus ½ cup (112 g) shredded mozzarella cheese, separated

1 tbsp. (3.84 g) dried parsley

1 egg for stuffing

Salt and pepper

14 oz. (397 g) marinara sauce

1 lb. (453 g) angel hair pasta

Directions:

Dip the eggplant slices in flour, then the beaten egg and milk mixture, then coat with bread crumbs. Heat the frying oil in a large skillet over medium high heat. Fry the eggplant on each side until golden brown. Remove to a paper-towel-lined plate to drain. Preheat the oven to 350 degrees F (175 degrees C).

Make stuffing with ricotta, 1½ cups (337 g) mozzarella, parsley, egg, salt, and pepper. Spread a thin layer of stuffing onto each slice of eggplant. Roll up tightly and place seam side down in a 9 x 13 (3.5 L) baking dish. Pour sauce over the rolls and top with the remaining shredded mozzarella cheese.

Bake for 45 minutes in a preheated oven until the cheese is melted and lightly browned. While the eggplant rolls are baking, bring a large pot of lightly salted water to a boil. Add the fresh angel hair pasta, and cook for 2 to 3 minutes, until tender. Drain. Serve eggplant rolls and sauce over pasta.

Luciana's Tiramisù

Tiramisù recipes began showing up around 1960 and were designed as a "lift-me-up" breakfast dish because *tiramisù* contains Italian coffee and eggs, but is now an evening dessert that has its origins in Venice or Treviso, depending on who you believe. It has turned into one of the most popular Italian desserts around the world.

Ingredients:

3 large eggs
2 tbsp. (14 g) powdered sugar
16 oz. (453 g) mascarpone cheese
2 tsp. (10 mL) vanilla extract
32 oz. (960 mL) heavy whipping cream
3 7.05 oz. PKGs (600 g) Italian Savoiardi lady fingers (a crunchy brand)
2 cups (475 mL) cold espresso
¼ cup (59 mL) spiced rum or coffee liqueur (optional)
1 oz. (28 g) powdered cocoa for dusting
dark chocolate (grated) for on top

Instructions:

Whip mascarpone cheese with 3 eggs and vanilla and place a thin layer on the bottom of a 13 x 9 x 2 (33 x 23 x 5 cm) baking pan. In a separate bowl, whip cream and powder sugar to stiff peaks. Mix the cold espresso with the rum (optional) and dip the lady fingers into the coffee just long enough to get them wet, do NOT soak them!

Arrange the lady fingers in the bottom of a baking dish (or container similarly sized). Spoon half the mascarpone cream filling over the lady fingers. Repeat with another layer of lady fingers. Mix remaining mascarpone cream with half of the whipping cream and spread over the lady fingers. Repeat with another layer of lady fingers. Spread the remaining whipping cream over the lady fingers (excess may remain). Sprinkle the top with powdered cocoa and shaved chocolate. Keep in the refrigerator for 8 hours or overnight before serving.

Baklava

Baklava is a popular Middle Eastern pastry. Many cultures claim it for their own, but most think the origins are Ottoman Turkish.

Ingredients:

16 oz. PKG (453 g) phyllo (filo) dough; thawed according to package instructions

1¼ cups (32 g) melted unsalted butter

4 cups (450 g) walnuts, finely chopped

1 tsp. (5.7 g) ground cinnamon

¼ tsp. (1.4 g) nutmeg

¾ cup (255 g) water

1 cup (201 g) granulated sugar

½ cup (170 g) honey

1 tsp. (5.7 g) vanilla

¼ cup (32 g) pistachio nuts, chopped (optional)

Directions:

Consider using forno paper or parchment paper to help prevent burning on the bottom of a 9 x 9 x 2 (23 x 23 x 5 cm) pan, and to protect the pan when you cut the pieces. Chop up the nuts with a food processor or knife and add cinnamon and nutmeg. Layer 6 to 8 sheets of phyllo dough in the pan, painting each piece with melted butter. Cover with half the nut mixture then layer 3 more sheets of buttered phyllo. Add the rest of the nut mixture and a top with 6 buttered sheets. I add chopped pistachios on top for taste and presentation.

Place the pan in the freezer or refrigerator to get the butter to harden. Then, take it out and cut the dough into the desired size pieces you want. (Phyllo dough with filling cuts easier when it is cooled. It's important to cut before you bake because otherwise it will crumble when you cut it.)

Place the pan on the bottom oven rack and bake at 350°F (177°C) for 11 minutes. While it bakes, add water, sugar, honey, and vanilla together in a saucepan and reduce on medium heat stirring constantly to reduce. When the top of the baklava is brown and crispy, remove from the oven and pour the hot reduction over the pan and into the cut lines, filling the pan with sticky goodness. You will hear it sizzle as it hits the hot pan. Yummy!

ACKNOWLEDGMENTS

A special thank you to Kurt Younker and his family for introducing me to an Italian, atypical tour with flair, and creating in me a desire for everyone to experience that type of vacation.

Anthony (Tony) Gaglio for being my biggest fan and advocate, and Mom and Dad for giving me my Italian/Sicilian heritage.

Thank you to my editing team Jane Saxton, Meghan Hoch, and editing consultant Gina Barresi, for helping me bring my heartfelt thoughts to print.

There have been many people along the way who have helped me make this transition through their support and encouragement, here are just a few: Catie Briggs, Cheryl Yeats, Roseann Gaglio, Michele Stephan, Angela & Anthony Mastrofrancesco, Candida Bing, Charles Matthew Webster, Jr., Robert & Carolyn Sherman, Steven & Susan Atkins, Tom & Susan Ghezzi, Dr. John A. DeCarolis, Emanuela Cucchiara, Eddie Morton, Susan A. Robinson, Pete Ronan, Mary Harper, Randolf Mikkelson, Sandra Lee Reeves,

Maurizio Matteuzzi, Kimberley Anne Pelyk, Larrie and Audrey Dahl, Haley Joyce Smith, Cheryl Lee Wyatt, John T. Glass & Carmen Lidia Pinheiro, Riccardo Mazzei, Karen Janet La Pensee, Deborah Louise Jacob, Stephanie Jean Trott, Joseph Muscatello, Edward & Christine Webler, Silvia Minardi, Rosaria Lupo, Loredana Cassigoli, Meghan Hoch, Jane Saxton, Steve Root, May Kay Capuano, Elaine Rutherford Clark, Alessia Montini, Loredana Crisafi, Elana Pietrunti, Cristina Amberti, Chiara Rozzi, Jeniffer Thompson, and Stephanie Thompson.

ABOUT THE AUTHOR

Robert Gaglio is an Italian chef, tour specialist, and educator. He founded Italian Culinary Tours in 2014. He is passionate about providing unique, authentic Italian tours that offer guests a deep cultural experience and a sense of what it's like to live like an Italian in all its richness. He splits his time between Italy and Florida.

DEAR READER

Thank you for taking this journey with me. If you enjoyed the book, please consider posting a review wherever you get your books.

I'd love to hear from you! Drop us a line. Perhaps you'll join me on a tour some day. Until then, enjoy each day to the fullest!

Goditi la vita al massimo!

—Robert M. Gaglio,

Italian Culinary Tours
www.ItalianCulinaryTours.com
Phone: (239) 223-4548
Email: contact@italianculinarytours.com

Manufactured by Amazon.ca
Bolton, ON

37554561R00114